ILLUMINATI INTUITION

TECHNIQUES AND PRACTICES TO MAXIMIZE YOUR SUPERNATURAL DECISION MAKING ABILITIES

THE ART OF USING YOUR IMAGINATION AND CREATIVE POWERS OF PRESCIENCE USING PSYCHOLOGY, SPIRITUALITY AND MBA SKILLS

GEORGE MENTZ JD MBA CILS

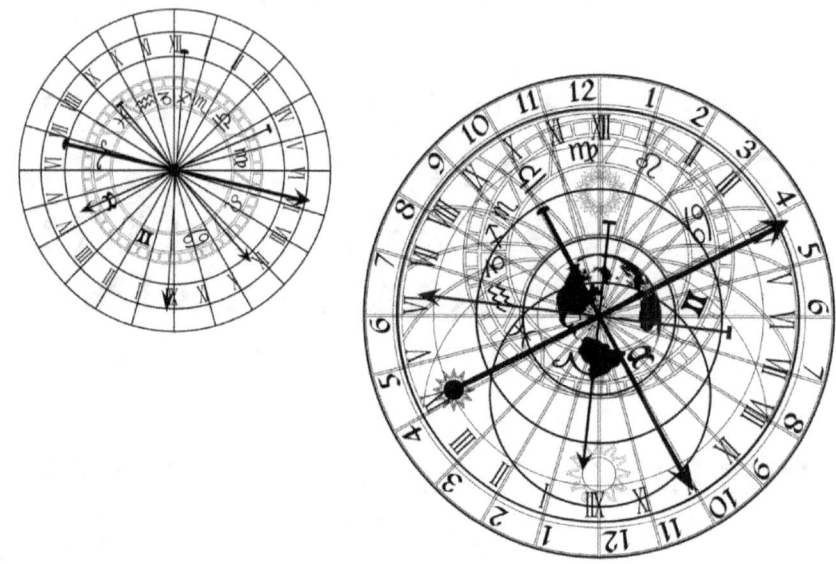

First published by
Mentzinger Media, LTD
http://www.gmentz.com
Endorsed by the Academy http://www.gafm.com
© George Mentz 2020
The right of George Mentz to be identified as the author of this work has been asserted in accordance with the Copyright, Designs and Patents Act 1988.
ISBN – Disclosed on Publishing
Library of Congress Cataloguing-in-Publication Data
Cataloguing in Publication Data
A catalogue record for this book is available online
 All rights reserved. No part of this manuscript or publication may be illegally copied, reproduced, stored in a retrieval system, or transmitted - in any form or by any means, electronic, mechanical, photocopying, recording and/or otherwise without the prior written express permission of the authors and or publishers. This book may not be lent, resold, scanned, hired out or otherwise disposed of by way of trade in any form, binding or cover

other than that in which it is published, without the prior consent of the publishers.

Printed in the USA from Mentzinger Media, LLC USA

All insights or content in this document is information of a general nature and does not address the circumstances of any particular family, individual or entity. Nothing in the Site constitutes professional advice, medical advice, or financial advice. Please consult a licensed professional before making any important decision. If you disagree with these Terms or are dissatisfied with this book or the author or the publication or publishing company, your sole and exclusive remedy is to discontinue using this book and its contents. Copyright 2020

Preface

In the last 20 years, I have consulted with billionaires and world leaders, and taught hundreds of business and law courses at accredited institutions as an award winning author and professor. Part of every successful relationship or career is based on sound decision making. During our lives, we will be put in the position of making critical decisions that affect our health, success, and peace of mind on a daily basis. The question is whether we can become better decision makers? Can we tap into that universal source of information that can help us make better choices. Can we become better at acquiring information, date and source information that can be used in our decision making processes. With all of that being said, we are all capable of having a more effective analytical mind. If you think of our minds as a machine, we all need to make sure it is running well, fueled for energy, is clear of debris, and is heightened with abilities from practice and prescience. The theme of this codex is how we all can be more in harmony, more efficient, more aware, more receptive, more intentional, more productive, and more successful.

There are several types of Intuitive Senses. These Clair-senses or Clairvoyance Types are for Decision Making Abilities :

1) Clairaudience can be messages of sound that you hear in your mind.

2) Clairsentient means clear feeling or clear feelings you receive from touching an object or person etc.

3) Claircognizance is when minds receive an immediate download from our intuition based on a question, idea, or flash of inspiration.

4) Clairvoyance means clear seeing which applies to all Clairs.

5) Clairalience means clear smelling.

6) Clairgustance means clear tasting.

Contents

Preface 3

The Magic of Intuition and Getting Clarity 10

What is Intuition and Magic? 15

Prosperity Teachings – The Mind and Good Luck 19

Some Mental Magic Observations 19

Thoughts Are Energy and Substance 23

   Our Thoughts, Actions, Inactions, and Omissions Create Our Receptivity and Character 23

Getting Clear & Purification Rituals 24

Getting Clear for Intuition Reception 26

The Holy Spirit or "God Force Energy" 31

A Course of Magic and Concepts to Perceptive Power: 38

15 Magical-Metaphysical Secrets to Power 38

The 15 MAGICAL SECRETS 40

   1. ILLUSION, ENERGY, & REALITY 40

   2. PERCEPTION 41

   3. UNITY 43

   4. THE PRESENT 43

   5. SPIRITUAL OPTIMIZATION 44

   6. POTENTIAL 45

   Quotes 45

   7. PURPOSE 46

   8. HARMONY 47

9. CREATIVITY 48

10. VISUALIZATION 49

11. CONTEMPLATION 50

12. ONGOING INVENTORY 51

13. CHARACTER 52

14. LOVE 53

    Quotes on Love 53

15. KNOWING 54

The Use of Imagination for Powerful Intuition 56

Intuition Exercises and Prescience Techniques 75

    Magical Guided Meditation – Consulting Your Holy Self 75

Exercises for Concentration, Intuition, Meditation, and Energy 77

Active Meditation Exercise 78

Exercise for Energizing or Healing Yourself. 79

Perception and Awareness Exercise 80

Affirmation Exercises 81

Prescience and Intuition 83

10 Exercises and Practices of Seeking Intuition, Prescience and Inspiration of Consciousness. 84

    1) Talk to Your Higher Self Exercise 84

    2) Magic Door Exercise 85

    3) Divining Symbols 85

    4) Contemplative Object 85

    5) Meditative Musing 86

    6) Look for Signs based on a Question 86

7) Pattern Writing	87
8) Imagine Decisions in the Future	88
9) Object Holding Exercise – Sense the Energy	88
10) The Papal Bowl of Intuition Exercise	89

In The Moment Intuition – Power of Inspiration 90

Exercises to Harness Your Passions in Life 90

Consciousness Exercises 93

10 Spiritual and Success Exercises...95

Spiritual Exercises To Expand Creativity, Prescience and Inspiration 100

1. Basic Prayers for Memory 100

2. Fellowship Exercise..100

3. Active Meditation 101

4. Seeking Inspiration and Prescience..101

5. Seeking God Consciousness 102

6. Mass as a Sacrament 102

7. Absorption Exercise: 103

8. Willingness Exercise: 104

9. Give It Away Exercise: 105

10. Character Analysis Ritual 106

11. Awareness Exercise: 107

12. Association Exercise: 107

13. Creativity: 108

14. Spiritual Gymnasium 108

15. Sacred Days..109

16. Services and Sacred Space 110

17.	Nature Bound and Pilgrimages and Commitments	110
18.	Communing with Yourself	111
19.	Catharsis and Purification	112
20.	Contemplative Action	113
22.	Meditative Objects	115
23.	Spiritual Jewelry and Charms	116
24.	Energy Centers	116
25.	Higher Self Visitation Exercises	117
26.	Mantras	118
27.	Prayer for Others and Forgiveness	118
28.	Hospitality Exercise	118
29.	Celtic Action	119
30.	Sabbath	119
31.	Environmental Exercise	120
32.	Character Exercise	120
33.	Tithe Exercise	121

The Process of Magic and Manifesting ... 122

The Power of Consciousness in the Now - Presumption Decoded ... 127

Being Contemplative in Action – Getting Into NOW ... 127

The Power of Esoteric Spirituality and Metaphysics ... 131

Power of Past and Present ... 138

Spiritual Filling and Re-Charging ... 138

Clear Your Mind – Banishing Negativity for Abundance ... 140

Prayers for Protection, Love, Forgiveness and Health ... 141

Acronyms to Inspire your Subconscious Mind ... 142

The 12 Characteristics of Prescient and Prosperous People 143

How to send and embed ideas in the Subconscious from Conscious. A Short List of Methods and Exercises? 144

Other Attributes that Affect and Change Belief Structure - Knowledge, Evidence, and Comprehension 146

The Elemental Mind and Body 147

The Mind of Wonder and Awe 149

Here are some steps that most people may find necessary to innovate, grow, expand, improve, or even heal 153

Steps needed to Make Big Changes 155

Spiritual Magic 156

    Various Steps in the Metaphysical and Magical World of Creativity, Good Fortune, Luck, Health, Wealth, and Success 156

Earth Wind and Fire 157

FIRE & HEAT 158

WATER & ICE 158

EARTH & SOIL 159

WIND & AIR 159

The Spirit of the Universe, The Force, All Pervading Ether or Ki Energy. ... 160

Psychic Defense & Talisman and Charms 161

About the Author 165

Bibliography: 166

The Magic of Intuition and Getting Clarity

1. The first step to practical intuition magic is to earnestly comprehend the beneficence and creative power of nature and the ever unfolding universe.

2. The second step is to go mentally from want to being receptively awake. So, we must go from wanting and being needy to becoming receptively alive and available for growth and prosperity to ideas, creation, and bold action.

3. The third step is to realize that abundance is good and good can come from increase and that we need prosperity to do good things for others. Also, we must realize that good people can do a lot of great things when they are empowered with peace, power, and prosperity.

4. Step four is to purify the mind and to banish negative thoughts. This begins by controlling the mind stream of thought. We must stop complaining and make the mental shift to thankfulness, gratitude and enthusiasm so that we can find inspiration and purpose with clarity.

5. The next step, step five, would be to turn your attention, intent and purpose, towards success and becoming who you truly want to be. To do this we need to free ourselves from the negative vibrations of ego mind and to free ourselves from self-loathing and self-nagging. This means that we should STRIVE to be in tune with our authentic self and embrace what makes us feel alive?

6. The next step is we need to clear and open our minds, our hearts and our hands to accept the gifts of life, the gifts of the universe, and gifts of abundance. To make a real transformation, we need to determine what we want to be, how we want to be, how we want to act, how we want to think. The applicable law here is, "to each according to their thinking, to each according to their essence", so we create our nature, and expand our inner essence according to what we aspire to be.

7. Begin to cultivate mindful flow of ideas and creativity. By clearing your mind, taking care of your body, and bettering yourself, you can then improve the dynamic flow of ideas, thoughts and dreams. The riches of the universe are composed of ideas, thought, innovation and action.

8. The next thought was we don't have to make huge and grandiose goals; we can have small steps that lead towards bigger goals. I would refer to this as an incremental process or a methodical magic. This step-by-step focus on our creativity via attainable goals will lead us to the path or to the destiny that we desire.

9. The eighth step would be to deeply think about the type of person that you really, really want to be. If you have to model yourself after somebody else, do that. You can always think of some great man or woman who you believe is wonderful, or who you idolize and think about the character traits that make them who they are. Consider the traits that you want to enjoy that would allow you to become a person of excellence. It could be character, it could be physical, it could be mental, it could be spiritual or a combination of all three, but the key is to change your vibration, to change your essence, to change who

you are by modifying what you are and becoming what you want to be.

10. The ninth step is to become super-receptive, which means to be completely aware of opportunities, be awake to the good in your life and be awake to the gifts coming to you with a thankful consciousness. So, if you are truly awakened, you are also allowing yourself to actually take advantage of opportunities that are sent your way. Thus, you see the signs or obtain the inspiration & understand the constructive insights that are needed to make decisions to head in the direction of your dreams.

11. The tenth step is to escape from a consciousness of lack and poverty. Many of us are taught that poverty is some type of piety, but it is not. Intentional or negligent styles of poverty causes more problems than anything else in the world. In poverty, you are unable to give as freely to those you love, you are unable to do many things for yourself and other people. So, what you want to do is change that consciousness from a perception of weakness to a view of strength. Thus, we must leave a consciousness of poverty to engage a new consciousness of wealth, health and mindfulness.

12. The next step would be to take a hard look at what's going on in your life, to basically stalk your own mind. Take a clear review of your track record and find out which things your mind-set does that you don't like and find out what type of ongoing consciousness would be the most constructive. The short-term goal is to find out what thoughts you have that are destructive. Weed out what is not productive so you can maximize your potential with ideas and attitudes that are creative and productive. As an example, when you are in need

of ideas and inspiration: try to relax, try to regroup, take a few deep breaths, slow yourself down and allow yourself to contemplate ANY good that's in your life RIGHT NOW, and allow yourself to be receptive to the CREATIVITY of the universe. Remember, all good that come to you must be blessed and ACCEPT all GOOD with thankfulness.

13. If you want to change your mental patterns, there is magic in making verbal DECREES to yourself. There is something supernatural in creating short affirmative rhymes and statements. This could explain why poetry based prayers have been around since the Sumerians created writing. Sometimes saying prayers or affirmations 3 times in a row adds power to these types of decrees. Affirmations are the ideas that you affirm to yourself to direct your conscious patterns of thought. Use these types of affirmations and decrees that are acceptable and believable to you and try to speak only of abundance and speak of truth to yourself.

14. As for your style of statements or affirmations, learn to say things to yourself like: "I am wealth", "I am health", "I am happiness", "I am joy", "I am getting better and better every day in every way", and when you say these things try and "see the decree". Try and see the declaration in your minds eye, and try and imagine how you would feel and how you would stand, how you would talk if you had the power that you are affirming. Try and imagine with your senses: your feelings, smell, sound, your hearing, taste, and sight. Try and visualize on all the different levels of sensory perception what it will be like to become WHO you want to be and "Feel it, and Internalize it, and Emotionalize it".

15. And then lastly, we all need to be in tune with the universe but also be Atoned with OUR internal universe as well. The

esoteric alignment of our inner vibration or essence with what we desire will alter our energy pattern to be a magnet for opportunity germane to our highest order. So, if you can try and maintain a harmonious relationship with yourself, the energy permeating the universe, the earth, with plants, with trees, with nature, with fire, with animals, with water/ice, & with the wind. Truly allow yourself to enjoy all of these things because the closer you are in harmony with all of the elements, the easier it will be to manifest on this material plane.

16. Doing it. Practice and Praxis. Engaging the world. Taking the next RIGHT step toward your fulfillment. Being what you want, doing what you want, and acting like your character or "excellence" depends on it.

What is Intuition and Magic?

First of all, I want to say no matter what you are doing in your life, whether you're working a job, taking care of your family, going to school, going to church on weekends, or exercising in the gym, there's magic involved in every bit of it in some way, shape or form. There is a mental and physical magical process to everything, and if you buy any book on the topic, whether it is on Celtic, Germanic or Egyptian magic, it doesn't matter what it is, there is a routine and a methodology to every act that seems magical. There are people that are experts at a particular activity. A specialist has invested tens of thousands of hours and they're masters at what they do. They use no mind. They just do. They can be and do at the same time because they inherently know the process and rituals of alchemy, imagination, awareness, receptivity, creativity, and prescience. What I'm talking about is the average person, whether you're in the military or in Silicon Valley or whether you're a priest or a rabbi, these everyday people are involved in some very high-tech routines on a daily basis that involve very scientific yet magical methodology. Some people call it project management while others might call it Chaos Theory/magic. Some people might call the process the Law of Attraction. Whatever you call it, there are concrete steps in any one of these ceremonies and tasks. Accordingly, the seeking of ideas and prescience is a practice, a type of prayer, a ritual, a technique, and a skill that can be developed.

Even if you walk into a typical Christian church service of today, there's going to be an opening ceremony, invocation, a procession, people walking in with various garments or sacred objects, going down the aisle, up to the altar where there are more sacred objects and tools that are used. There's singing. There are decrees that are involved. People may read psalms or prayers at the beginning of the service. They may be readings that involve the Bible or even some other literature and the people may engage in a ritual of self purification where the participants ask for forgiveness, grace and blessings. Then, many seekers may actually participate in what is called a communion and that is where the congregations is receiving "bread and wine" which is considered the body and blood of the Savior of the Christian church which is Jesus The Christ or "The Great Master". Why do I bring all this up? Because, there is a method to all activity and sacred practice. If you watch during any typical Christian service where there is communion involved, they are using consecrated space, there is an individual who is ordained who is at the altar working with the tools and preparing or "charging" the gifts and invoking the power and the energy of God into those gifts to share with the people.

We witness a special act of grace where the act itself is magical, something that provides awe, then there's nothing else like that. It's an extraordinary ancient ritual where each person in the congregation proceeds up, shares this gift and becomes connected to the "Source of All Good".

On the other hand, if you went to any classic lodge meeting or even a club of people who gather every so often, they will open those types of meetings with some very special routines, group movements, and rituals. They may recite the Pledge of Allegiance. They may say a prayer with a leader involved. They may use Robert's Rules of Order, and they may discuss certain issues according to the planned or itemized schedule. Every major organization has its methods but what is interesting about the ancient lodges and temples of the world is that the physical design and setup is based on the Cardinal Points and the buildings and rooms face in certain directions, much like churches. Churches, temples and other religious buildings generally are designed to be facing certain directions where the entrance of the building is facing a certain way such as NORTH and so forth. On the inside, they may have preordained places for special seats for particular individuals of the organization. That could be the same whether it's any religious institution or otherwise, or some type of lodge for instance.

What is truly magical is whether you're in the military or in a lodge or at a church, most people will be moving around the interior of those facilities or the sacred space in a very orchestrated and special way according to either ancient rituals or some type of special movements that have been followed for a very long time. On the inside of a lodge or some type of religious facility, people will be either reciting or saying certain statements or lectures that are there to either teach people or where people are actually saying things out loud to petition the respective power or intercessions of the universe for blessings, good fortune or assistance. With all of that being said, you have to admire any custom where people go in and praise the universe, ask for blessings, ask for forgiveness, commune with each other, sing songs of joy and prayers and are lifted up with lectures about ethics, virtues and love or the path to become a better person. All of that really makes sense in the big scheme of things for living your best life.

I think there is magic to ALL of these Activities. There is magic to helping adults participating in these things but there's also a magic in children being raised in an environment where they can learn as well as engage in the art of participating in these very special rituals. There is magic to learning prayers and affirmations. There is also something supernatural to owning special items such as gems, amulets, prayer cards, figures of saints, religious jewelry and charms. Many people even collect rocks from various religious or spiritual sites from around the world.

So what is magic? It's everywhere. Like I said, even if you're on the job in Silicon Valley and you've got a team of people and you're involved in a project, you're going to have to sit down with the team and say, "What are we doing? What is our directive? How do we diagnose this situation? How do we move forward? How do we develop a plan? How do we implement that plan? How do we monitor and continuously improve on what we're doing, become a better team, work with each other, help each other and make the organization bigger or stronger and healthier so you can provide goods and services to help your community or help the world be a better place?" That is magic. There is magic in that. It's just like von Goethe said, "There is magic in it when you begin it." All of us need to commence engaging the magic of life. When we have great ideas, the hardest part is beginning them and implementing them so that the nucleus of energy begins its action and begins moving. Once that movement starts, great things happen and there is magic in everything that we do. When our willingness and intent are focused in any direction, we begin to manifest our destiny. However it must be noted that, there are many ways to clear our space, purify our minds, concentrate our will, enhance our beliefs, and expound upon our knowingness of potential success. This book is about using our spoken word, tapping into our willpower, and cultivating our spiritual energy with special exercises, tools, and timeless knowledge.

Prosperity Teachings – The Mind and Good Luck

Some Mental Magic Observations

It seems that the whole dynamic message contained in prosperity teachings hinges on the concept of ideas, mind and mind stuff that can propel energy or communication. However, to work with the forms of mind stuff, the individual consciousness must have a stream of something called thought. Random thought can be a waste of energy and time for all involved. However, thought that is inspired by ideas has great power. Thought with purpose, feeling, and concentration is even more energized.

As we must remember, when we connect to and activate the supernatural MIND within, we are inspired with the divine ideas of: innovation, change, growth, and creation. Acting and seizing upon this new 6th sense that is tied to your natural expressive self is the KEY to right livelihood, effort, and action. Stop fighting and resisting growth and your potential. You and your constructive dreams and ideas ARE your purpose and wealth RIGHT NOW. Your consciousness is YOUR UNIQUE unlimited supply of being and creative substance.

When a person stops struggling and initiates ALCHEMY OR MAGIC, SOMETHING HAPPENS. An openness and willingness appears. It is energy of great force. Hope is good because it signifies an openness to surrender to something greater which many persons refer to the supernatural energy of faith power. To transcend struggle and hope is to begin singing the praises of creation. Discouragement, frustration, blame and justified anger drain great amounts of spiritual energy from anyone. To choose a new "world view" takes great effort but this choice soon becomes a skill of discernment. To develop this skill, we must overcome laziness and self-anointed victimhood as soon as possible. However, much like a mental gymnasium, any man or woman can begin a shift of consciousness with practice and open-mindedness. A consciousness with a bedrock foundation of gratitude, acceptance, peace, willingness, and desire can lead to a real shift toward tangible belief and conviction.

It is not the quantity of spirituality – it is the quality of Faith and Knowingness. Even if part of your conscious has doubt of fear, the small and unshakable foundation of faith will immunize your SELF from false appearances. As we all know, a tiny amount of light prevents darkness from existing and your inner light will invariably grow if you allow it and are willing to receive it. Meet the universe half-way with good cheer and a world view backed by love, thanks and praise, and the heavens will continue to shower you with abundance and opportunity to serve humanity.

The reason for studying these concepts is this. You can render no greater service to humanity than to make the most of yourself. Without a proper view of yourself and the world of opportunity in life, you may never begin to engage life and living in a way to maximize the fullness of your existence. Because poverty and ignorance generally interfere with freedom and love, we begin to ask all who read these teachings if you are ready to recreate your world and reinvent your soul essence.

On this physical plane, we see that like causes do IN FACT creates like effects. With this law, if you engage actions of belief, focus, imagery, visualization, decrees, prayers, affirmations, or even charging symbols, you are magnetizing results in your favor. Thus, if we desire a certain result, we use the method or formula that proves most effective. So, most people recognize that a recipe has certain ingredients, but most in this world do not comprehend that CREATION and TRUE Success has certain mental and spiritual ingredients also.

Nature itself is responsive to your mind. It is an undeniable fact. The original or primordial substance can be molded by spiritual mind. Because we have not achieved the advanced stages of our spiritual evolution, we are working now in the beginning phases of cognitive transcendence and mastery, but even at this stage, an average person can become endowed with more power that then had ever hoped and wished for.

Without perfect manifestation, we are using the strategies that allow advance creation. These tactics are spiritual in nature, but dramatically speed up progress on both the physical and spiritual plane for anyone who is willing to use them.

- Begin NOW to cultivate your burning desires and life's purpose. (Things that you truly want to do and are willing to commit wholeheartedly to). You can also refer to this as your intentions and goals. Make a list of things you want to achieve and begin honing you plans and objectives. Make a list of things about yourself that you want to improve, and begin to think about these also.
- Simply allow yourself believe in one Intelligent Substance where you express thankful acknowledgement. The universe wants to help you, it has unlimited supply, and only desires your cooperation by meeting it ½ way.
- Realize that what you desire is available to be yours with Grateful Heartfelt Emotion and Faith and you only need to say the word to have it begin to become manifest.
- Form a blueprint of what you desire in your mind and on your mental picture screen. See it each and every day and allow it to

be cultivated and specific in nature.
- Give you attention wholly to prosperity, great ideas, and thoughts of creation.
- Since Belief is All Important, it best serves you to stay away from people, places and entertainment that you know will interfere with your Constructive Path and Affirmative Consciousness. Quit struggling and start: Doing and Being.
- Do all you can each day without haste or hurry that leads to the completion of your goals or desires. Do things one at a time as best you can.
- Allow your ideas to flow. Set your intentions. Pick what you want to do in life, and allow your intuition and decision making powers to flow. Take notes, analyze your ideas, pick the ideas that feel best to you in your gut, do your research, and try to achieve your goals in relation to this flow of creative ideas.
- Do not focus on the poverty and ills of the world. Take action to protect and improve yourself. You will then be able to help others all you want after you have become truly prosperous on the inside and out.

Thoughts Are Energy and Substance

Our Thoughts, Actions, Inactions, and Omissions Create Our Receptivity and Character

Overall, if we desire prosperous and peaceful energy, we must be willing to put out good thoughts, praise others, become thankful, see things in an opportunistic light, and have faith in the regeneration of mind and body. Our every action and thought of goodness is very powerful. Acts of kindness, service to others, and self-development are all extremely powerful energies. Negative feelings are feeble thoughts that are a hundred times less powerful than acts of creation and constructiveness.

If we maintain a harmonious relationship with others while keeping a peaceful relationship with ourselves, then life can be much easier where our awareness and receptivity to flow is greatly enhanced.. Further, when we are avoiding wasteful thinking and actions, our spiritual energies may maintain their laser focus and power. As with physics, it is possible to neutralize a sound wave by setting up another sound wave of the same pattern that comes from the opposite pole. Therefore it is possible to conjure and visualize ideas, thoughts, and images that can completely neutralize old attitudes. By changing your outlook, you can change your future. Every cause has its effect, and every action has its results, but it is desire that is the link that connects the two. Thinking on a higher level requires a mind that is free, lean, efficient, harmonious, and clear. Gratitude and attunement will afford us the clarity to absorb prosperity and build anew.

Getting Clear & Purification Rituals

This exercise can be done before you do any type of really purposeful prayer, purposeful meditation or purposeful ritual, whatever it may be. The reason for doing this is for purification, and it could be called a generalized banishing ritual. (To protect your prayer space, protect your mind, and allow effective a connection your Spirit to the Universe.)

To begin with, take a few deep breaths through your nose, breathe out your mouth, and imagine your whole body is surrounded by a white light. Imagine a white light starting in your heart and blazing out through your entire body, and then surrounding your entire body like an orb, like a big circle around your entire body and your entire soul that's surrounding you and protecting you. Then, imagine that white light shooting down through your dominant arm, whether it's left or right, it doesn't matter. And as that light goes into your hand, you can either imagine it or do it physically if you want if you're in a safe, quiet place and move your hand around your body in a circle horizontally. And then you can imagine moving your hand around you perpendicularly in a full circle.

Then, with your hand again, make another circle around your body. But, make it over your top right down to your bottom left a full circle, and then with your hand again, over your top left and over your bottom right, make another circle. The objective is, is to make four circles around your body – perpendicular, horizontal, and then north, northeast, and northwest over you. And in these circles, you create almost the da Vinci effect or like an electron energy that is flowing around your body in circles protecting your body. And when you're finished doing this, you're actually protecting your entire heart, mind, and soul from any negative energy coming into it. And the wonderful thing about this is that in your imagination, you can pull your family into this circle that surrounds your body. The circle can be enlarged enough to where it surrounds your entire home and surrounds your family, your children, your spouse, your loved ones. They're all with you in your imagination. And this is done to protect everyone close to you and including yourself.

At this time after purifying your space, you make your prayer, affirmation decree to charge or energize something with your focused intent.

All of those types of exercises can be done after you've gone into this specialized protected alpha state. So your mind is calm and your body is protected from all outside intrusion.

Alternatively, if you prefer a 7 direction exercise that some Native Americans have practiced, that is also a great way to clear out our space.

Getting Clear for Intuition Reception

The Course of Intuition contains many insights, ideas, and paths to obtain peace, love and forgiveness. One of the fundamental messages of the Course is the difference between reality and illusion and what is true about the way we think and what is false. For personal mastery, we must be able to identify what is part of our ego and what is part of our authentic self, or our spiritual self. The key to this first teaching is that nothing can really hurt what is inside of you, the real authentic you, your real spiritual self. Nothing can hurt that. No matter what happens to your physical body, there is a part of you that can never be hurt, which is part of the "Spirit of the Universe" and part of God. To really come into a knowing-ness of this teaching, you must believe that you are connected to the source of creation and that you are a child of creation. Once you can deeply feel that connection between your spirit and the universe, then you are linked with that connection where you can finally reach your authentic power and your potential.

Now we realize that it may be difficult for many of you to believe in a power greater than yourself or a God of your understanding can be a challenge for some people, however, it must be said that if you can embrace the principles or the path, or you can embrace the spiritual philosophy and the love of the universe. The key, honestly, is acknowledging that you are not god, and you are not in total control. I understand that can be a hard thing to swallow for some, but when you let go and allow the universe to be your guide and to cooperate with The G-FORCE, you receive POWER. That means you are deliberately and intently and mutually operating with and in the universe. You find it is easier not playing god, and you understand that the universe is the greater force that you can cultivate for your advantage. As soon as you begin to cooperate with that force and that concept, then you can become harmonious with the creative power. To cultivate flow or be in tune with the spirit and unified with it, that is the Quantum Leap to obtain enthusiasm and empowerment. The second step is about reality and trying to attack it or protect yourself or separate from it. The ego is constantly talking to you, trying to protect your ego-self from other people, to make yourself feel better about yourself or sometimes it's trying to make you feel worse about yourself. The secret is to transcend that false ego and let go of that ego mind and self talk that is not real, it's just ego-chatter-based opinions. By letting go and learning to filter, you can connect with that spiritual self and your mind will no longer be a "house divided."

That real self is authentic and that real self knows that you ARE a good and whole and complete perfect being. Unfortunately for many of us, the ego is driven by pride, lust, anger, greed, gluttony, envy and sloth. Ego is even driven by subtle discouragement or justifiable resentment. So this false-mind and ego needs this ego-food to empower itself and the key for us to live happily and efficiently and effectively is to quit feeding the ego with this type of negative nutrition that it loves.

This separation between us as spiritual children from "A God of our understanding" is a fallacy in the clouded mind. The key to spiritual power is to clear away the wreckage of the past, to clear away the mental garbage, to dissipate the pride and the anger and the greed and the discouragement and the resentment, to let all of that go, push it aside, work through it, talk to other people about it, pray about it. Pray for those in our past, to let go of them. Do these things to receive this gift of cleansing and catharsis so we can reconnect to our Christ selves or our holy spirit.

Thus, the Magical Strategy IS the connection SECRET. Getting away from the separation and reconnecting to spiritual power is available for everyone who earnestly and sincerely wants it because it's always there. The miracle of unity is always available, the gift is always ready for those who are willing to accept it, but all of us must open our hearts and open our closed fists to receive this celestial reward.

Many hold on to old ideas and grievances. Many of us believe that we have sinned or that we have been bad people in the past, that we've done unforgivable harms. The real question of the day is will your God forgive you? Can you forgive yourself? And the answer is yes to both, if you are willing to allow yourself to be forgiven, if you are willing to forgive others and if you are willing to forgive God and if you are willing to allow God to forgive you. Then this forgiveness, this peace of mind, this peace that passeth all understanding can be available to you. It may take a little work but you can work through it. If you need help, you can always find a licensed counselor, a life coach, a priest, rabbi or an imam or even someone in a 12 step program. You can discuss privately these topics one-on-one and through private discourse. Also, you may discuss other important issues with your god of your personal understanding so that you may gain this peace and let go of these alleged sins. The objective is to put past ideas *which may be draining your energy* in the past because you need this purity of mind, this clarity of mind so you can stay connected and operate at a higher order of being.

There comes a point where all of us have an ego-voice that wants to blame others or use resentments to justify ourselves or justify the way we feel about other people. We were trying to blame people, places and things for the way we feel about ourselves, or we're trying to blame people and institutions for our failures. Or, we're trying to use our resentments, blame or anger to justify our guilt or to understand our shame. But there comes a point where each and every one of us needs to let go of our shame. There comes a point where all of us have to say, "Nobody can shame me anymore, nobody can shame the authentic spiritual self that you have inside you."

In many religions, there comes a point where you become reborn, reinvented, reconnected or even re-baptized as an adult and your faith becomes alive again. With faith and earnest beliefs, you transcend hope and knowingness. You can achieve this higher level of real belief and faith. Ultimately, if you can cultivate and develop faith, that is where real happiness and real peace of mind comes from, because you've altered your thought patterns to a higher dimension.

In spiritual programs, you might hear someone talk about a spiritual awakening, becoming awake spiritually or even developing a sixth sense or higher consciousness. In some of philosophies where people may NOT believe or recognize a god, there are countless seekers who have cultivated faith and belief in conjunction with a power greater than themselves which could be the principles, path, or other set of devout values. To continue to grow spiritually, we need to work on what's called inner social justice or inner spiritual growth. Thus, if you are part of a spiritual program, it is contingent upon every one of us to build ourselves from the inside out using what is called "Inner Justice". Working on forgiveness, love, meditation, and love, we can continue to be in tune with the universe and solve our inner conflicts. This spiritual exercise allows us to maintain a harmonious relationship with ourselves, with God, with other people while improving self love, self regard, and love for the universe.

This is an extremely important magical and alchemical process, so let me say it one more time. The most important relationships you can cultivate is the one with yourself and your relationship with the force of the universe. By improving these mental concepts, you retrain your brain, create new empowering neuro-pathways, and the way you perceive yourself and your environment will dramatically improve.

The Holy Spirit or "God Force Energy"

What is that to us? Many people who have been reborn or reinvented in their faith because they have felt the spark of the inner Christ within them which may be called a reconnection. To put it into a simple allegory, let's pretend that there is a small fuse within your mind and that fuse can be blocked with emotions such as: anger and resentment or pride or jealousy or greed. All of these ills, what we would call deadly sins, affect the function of this "inner fuse of light".

Once you can clear out some of these blockages, like resentment, jealousy, anger or discouragement, the fuse lights up. And, that burning light is your connection between your spiritual self and the inner Christ which connects you to the source of all there is. This energy, enthusiasm, and the aliveness is the Holy Spirit, and that is what you hear people talk about who have been awakened.
It's a third force. It's you, the universe and something in-between that is a bright, magical connection and you know it when you have it. This inner awakening process does take persistence, but if you ask the universe to be connected to it, the power will materialize. If you ask for the release from bondage from self and from ego and ask for release from resentments and anger, blame, guilt and shame, then, you will know freedom. By doing all of these other things and allowing yourself to be set free, the inner-burning, bright, shining connection can be yours.

Some people might call this bright light a "spiritual awakening" or some people might refer to this in A Course of Miracles as the "holy instant", a moment where your connection is realized and you know you are cooperating or participating with a power greater than yourself fueled by love and where the ego is not controlling you. Then we can heal our perception by individually forgiving the world. We can change our hearts and minds when we decide earnestly to expand the way we think by asking ask the universe for help and by praying to receive this gift of a superior perception. Then, we can become awakened and alive and aware for truly the first time.

Changing our minds about the world and allowing the Holy Spirit to heal the way we feel, to heal our worldview, to heal the way we think is ultimately the key to freedom. And, once you embrace this Holy Spirit or this spiritual awakening, then you will have this expanded perception.

But first, you need to remember that you must clear away the mental debris of the past create fresh, empty space within your heart and within your mind – for new LIFE , for new and good and wholesome beliefs. Once you have cleared away the old ideas and made room for some good, then the spirit of the universe lights up within you, this inner Christ and this inner connection to the Holy Spirit and the universe becomes alive. You, in turn, become energized and then the way you view the world at any given moment becomes clear and augmented. If you have a consciousness of wealth or a consciousness of happiness or a consciousness of peace, at any given moment, it will then color the way you perceive that moment and the way you give purpose and meaning to your life.

There are many ways to heal our perceptions, but one of the best methods is to renew the mind, forgive yourself, to forgive other people and to forgive God. We do this because, let's face it, there are two relationships that are most important in your life – the relationship with youself and the relationship with a power greater than yourself which most simply call GOD. These two relationships can make or break you. Those two relationships can make life easy or make life a struggle and as many spiritual programs profess, struggle is not necessary. Needless struggle is not mandatory. A lot of people, a lot of us, want to hold onto these old ways, hold onto these old habits, this old way of thinking because it gives us adrenaline and it makes us feel better than other people. It allows us to forget about our failures when, in fact, if we could let go of negative thinking and let go of these destructive habits, then our authentic selves can blossom and we can become who we really are meant to be. Further, we can become connected and have this intuition and this creativity that we're really supposed to utilize that makes us feel alive, that makes us feel authentic, and that makes us feel like we have purpose. Finally, we will then feel that we are truly heading down the path that we were always meant travel.

If you are having trouble with forgiveness, then we can offer several different methods to fix that problem or to cure that problem. The first one is every day when you wake up and every night before you go to bed, start saying affirmations aloud or to yourself or even in the mirror. You can write your own affirmations or you can go to the store and buy a book on affirmations and prayers to read silently or aloud. Many read these prayers or these meditations to themselves, or even read them out loud or to another person who loves and supports you.

Some may read them in conjunction with working with a spiritual counselor, sponsor, or a life coach. Read affirmative literature each day in the morning and in the evening and your beliefs and your worldview will change. Your vibration and energy will be altered upward. Your mindset will be enhanced and you will obtain a sense of excellence and poise.

Sometimes it takes 30 days before you even feel a major change or a major effect, but it will come quickly and powerfully. You may not even notice it but I promise you that if you do these practical-magical exercises for 30 days where you focus on gratitude, on peace of mind, & on forgiveness, you will become spiritually free and empowered.

If you have problems even beyond that, challenges even that you think are too heavy for basic prayers and affirmations, I recommend that you hit your knees every morning and every night and you ask directly to the God of your understanding for help. Or, you simply ask the Holy Spirit or Jesus Christ or ask your favorite Saint for intercession or assistance. It doesn't need to be perfect, as you simply need to humble yourself and tune in to the SOURCE and ask if you can be assisted and offer to cooperate. That's it. You will be amazed with the power you receive. The key is that you earnestly make petition direct to God and say, "Please forgive me, please heal me, please remove my resentments, and please take away my dislike or my hatred for this person or for myself."

Or you may even pray for the happiness of another person or other individual, you pray earnestly and ask God to bless them and to take them away from your thinking. Ask your higher power to bless everyone, to bless those in your family, in your household, but most importantly, ask for grace for yourself, ask for peace for yourself, and ask for a thankful heart for yourself. Become a person who praises other people or even blesses your very self. Become a person who speaks of constructive and grateful and thankful things and if you do all of this, you will have what is called a grateful heart. You will have a firm belief and faith in the universe because it will change your faith in mankind. Many of us have had some really tough challenges. An example might be the death of someone close in your family or a family member or a great sickness or a catastrophic event such as a hurricane or a tsunami, whatever it might be. Some of us may have experienced a business divorce, a family divorce, your parents divorcing, or even yourself. All of these things can be extremely challenging and when we get into these situations that are extremely challenging, it's a call for many of us to rise to the occasion and become stronger.

Many times, we are going to have to release the other people that are involved whether it's a business problem with a partner or a lawsuit or a divorce or even a situation with our children. We're going to have to release people, release them with love, pray for them, pray that we can forgive them, and pray that they can forgive us. If we are able to do these things and to let go of what's hurting us and to become free and awake and aware while in forgiveness, all of these things provide us a true perception. This authentic perception looks past the bodily illusion to the light of Christ, and we will begin to see the little bit of God that is in all people. When we finally reach this spiritual awake-ness and clarity, then the Holy Spirit will lift us up and make us whole. However, there is an investment that we have to make in maintaining this spiritual condition and a lot of it comes by using a basic methodology and some fundamental tools herein.

So to maintain our spiritual condition, we're probably going to need to do spiritual things and act responsibly. What we mean by that is to respond in a spiritual way to life and if that becomes difficult, of course, then you will have to continue to work the steps hitherto and continue to integrate the healthy virtues and ethics of the philosophy of your understanding or archetype.

We practice these spiritual exercises to maintain clarity, to maintain forgiveness, to maintain some sense of purity of mind. Purity of mind is where you are acting with love and unselfishness and you have a mindset of clear-and-convincing gratitude. That's what we mean by purity of mind and if you're doing things on a daily basis to maintain this quality of mind and quality of spirit and quality of perception, then that inner Christ, that inner light will remain bright and protect you because you will be acting in concert and in cooperation with the pure force of creation.

Similarly, many of us will need to deeply consider how we can continue to look at our character development. We enhance our character by observing the way we're acting, not acting, and the ways we're thinking. Maybe at the end of the day, take some notes about how you acted and think about ways that you can become a better person. Even 200+ years ago, Benjamin Franklin, in his autobiography, talked about his devotion to this evening practice of taking an inventory of his day with the motive of trying to become a better person tomorrow.

By prayer and meditation and maintaining this sufficient humility of which we've talked about, we will maintain some sense of clarity and spirituality in our lives. What we mean by humility are 4 key attributes: that you understand that you are teachable; that you understand your true authentic place in this world; that you are connected to a power greater than yourself; and that you understand who you really are. Humility is really the opposite of the insane ego-driven grandiosity or self-defeating thinking that inhibits our happiness. These practices are designed to eliminate the blocks to your connection to the spirit. If we desire to maintain our spiritual condition, then what will be important is our dedication to prayer, meditation, humility, clarity, love, and forgiveness. By virtue of our efforts, we become operative at a higher order and this higher state blesses us with a unity to a power greater than ourselves. Then, we finally understand our true identity and our sonship with God.

By using these 15 steps below, you will cultivate the mindset and harmonious spiritual nature that is necessary to be tuned into the Great Spirit or Great Consciousness. Some great psychologists such as Dr. Carl Gustav Jung call it the collective consciousness, other great anthropologists such as Pierre Teilhard de Chardin call it the Noosphere of thought.

Whatever we call it, every idea comes from somewhere and many folks have the clarity of intellect to receive and cultivate amazing ideas which completely shift the fortunes of individuals and even humanity.

A Course of Magic and Concepts to Perceptive Power:

15 Magical-Metaphysical Secrets to Power

The course in Magic is a process of metaphysics and spiritual transformation. If one engages in certain activities, thinking, practices, action, and omissions, then the seeker can grow rapidly. Through a process of trial and error, most people have found that a spiritual lifestyle of harmony is the easier, softer way of growth. The concepts herein are the keys to transformation which will allow the reader to transcend limitations. The goal is that you are able to get past your preconceptions, expand past what is apparent and develop into who you were meant to become.

Getting past the illusions of ego and realizing your true self can be magical and miraculous. When we are able to realign our consciousness with the SOTU "The Spirit of the Universe", then you will be able to put your spiritual life before ego mind. Removing blocks and becoming awake to our spiritual self allows for this supernatural connection to flourish.

As for the "Spiritual Mechanics", this is a process of tuning in with the infinite. This tuning in creates a divine flow and connection which gives us the *peace that passeth all understanding.* If we focus on certain constructive action, concepts and ideas, we then reap the benefits of such activity. In simple terms, if we can master constructive actions and thinking, we will become masters of our destiny.

Many spiritual movements contain ideas and exercises that are based in the ancient religious and ethical traditions. These principles assist in our transformation and reinvention. Thus, we can become much greater people if we can get tuned in with our spiritual essence, go through a catharsis to clear the mind and soul, build our character, learn to live with more efficient thinking through forgiveness. Then we live in the consciousness of love, peace, and prosperity. This is what can be referred to as a rebirth or personal reincarnation.

As with Paul's letters to the Corinthians, love has many facets, such as patience, kindness, generosity, humility, courtesy, unselfishness, good temper, guilelessness, and sincerity. Gratitude is also a major ingredient to the successful equation of love, peace, and abundance. If we can master these timeless virtues, we benefit, and ALL people profit in our proximity from the ripple effect of our living in a higher order of existence. As Thoreau said, *"If one advances confidently in the direction of his dreams, and endeavors to live the life which he has imagined, he will meet with a success unexpected in common hours. He will put some things behind, will pass an invisible boundary; new, universal, and more liberal laws will begin to establish themselves around and within him; or the old laws be expanded, and interpreted in his favor in a more expansive sense, and he will live with the license of a higher order of beings."*

The 15 MAGICAL SECRETS

Please review these 15 secrets to Power. Ponder the concepts and meaning of he following chapter and quotes. Then, cultivate a willingness to engage any of these practices which may give you greater prosperity, freedom and peace of mind.

1. ***ILLUSION, ENERGY, & REALITY*** -- We are living in the illusion where we are separated from our divine inheritance of being spiritually awake. Our goal is to regenerate our souls through this PROCESS, and realize that the spirit/self that lies within us is the divine connection that propels us to our natural and highest livelihood. This separation limits our abilities as we are limited by our ego-mind. Evaluating our history and track record with honesty we can see that we have much more potential. We then should learn how to grow and leave behind unproductive living and attitudes. How can we head toward wholeness, peace and prosperity? Through transformation and optimization of mind, one can meet their true inner Self which is connected to the Spirit of the Universe. We are all part of the Force or Spiritual Energy of The Universe. Without our spirit, our mind and bodies would not be animated, filled with ideas, and alive. We become awake spiritually and realize that all is right with our world, and we apply the highest and most constructive truth to our world view.

- "There are as many pillows of illusion as flakes in a snow-storm. We wake from one dream into another dream. " Ralph Waldo Emerson
- *A wise man, recognizing that the world is but an illusion, does not act as if it is real, so he escapes the suffering. – The Buddha*

- "Neither shall they say, Lo here! or, lo there! for, behold, the kingdom of God is within you." (Luke 17:21)
- "The real self (*atman*) is distinct from the temporary body. One must go beyond the illusion of ego and self, to find their true essence and soul." ~ Magus Incognito
- The Bhagavad-Gita states our atman... the supreme consciousness that invades whole cosmic system is the only truth of life! Our atman soul is the truthful master and controller of body.
- "Sometimes, simply by sitting, the soul collects wisdom." ~Zen proverb
- Fantasies are the veil behind which truth is hidden. (ACIM p. 316)
- "Don't be satisfied with stories, how things have gone with others. Unfold your own myth." — Rumi, Essential Rumi

2. **PERCEPTION** – GRATITUDE, ENTHUSIAM, AND OPTIMISM - Our aliveness and well being is based on our spiritual condition which is based on the operative, optimal – mechanics of our mind (ability to see and perceive). At present, we are limited to the primitive view of only that which is surface reality and apparent, and we must evolve to be able to see beyond what is obvious. Liberation takes effort; thus, "A better view generates a better journey".

Quotes:
- Finally, brethren, whatsoever things are true, whatsoever things are honest, whatsoever things are just, whatsoever things are pure, whatsoever things are lovely, whatsoever things are of good report; if there be any virtue, and if there be any praise, think on these things. Philippians 4:8

- "The first gulp from the glass of natural sciences will turn you into an atheist, but at the bottom of the glass God is waiting for you." — Werner Heisenberg – World Renowned Physicist
- The mind can be the source of bondage, or can be the source of liberation. (Maitri Upanishad)
- Come to me, all who labor and are heavy laden, and I will give you rest. Take my yoke upon you, and learn from me, for I am gentle and lowly in heart, and you will find rest for your souls. For my yoke is easy, and my burden is light." Matthew 11:28-30
- The cessation of the discriminating mind cannot take place until there is a "turning-about" in the deepest seat of consciousness.

The Lankavatara Sutra – Buddha

- In gathering your vital energy so that you can create agility, have you achieved the state of a new-born child? In cleansing your inner vision, have you purified all of its dullness? Lao Tzu
- Unless one is born anew he will not be able to see the kingdom of God...unless one is born of water and the Spirit, he cannot enter the Kingdom of God. That which is born of flesh is flesh. That which is born of spirit, spirit is.

The Gospel of John – Jesus Christ

- All things born in truth must die, but out of death comes life.

The Bagavad Gita - Krishna

3. **UNITY** - To connect to the power of the universe, we must be fined tuned into our individual spirit which connects us to the Divine Flow of the Universal Spirit. - Through a catharsis, purification, forgiveness, we obtain wholeness and clarity.

   Quotes
   - When practicing contemplation, They should wish that all beings, See truth as it is. And be forever free of oppression and contention.
   - Buddhism. *Garland Sutra, 11*
   - Lord of Creation! No one other than Thee pervades all these that have come into being. May that be ours for which our prayers rise, may we be masters of many treasures!
   - Hinduism. *Rig Veda, 10.121.10*
   - If the poorest of mankind come here once for worship, I will surely grant their hearts' desire.
   - Shinto. *Oracle of Itsukushima*
   - "But seek ye first the kingdom of God and His righteousness," he declared, "and all these things shall be added unto you."
   - (Matthew 6:33).
   - *"Be the change that you wish to see in the world."*
   - *Mahatma Gandhi*

4. **THE PRESENT** - Cultivating positive energy, we tune in and obtain connectedness which affords us divine flow, ideas, and clarity. Our inner voice is clear when our mind is clear. This transparency allows for better decisions in seizing upon your ideas.

   Quotes
- Jesus said to him, "No one who puts his hand to the plow and looks back is fit for the kingdom of God." ~ Luke 9:62

- "If you are depressed, you are living in the past. If you are anxious, you are living in the future. If you are at peace, you are living in the present." ~ Lao Tzu
- "Not what we have But what we enjoy, constitutes our abundance." ~ Epicurus (Greek philosopher, B.C. 341-270)
- Do not dwell in the past, do not dream of the future, concentrate the mind on the present moment. ~ Buddha
- Our wealth is rewarded in direct proportion to the number of people with whom we are willing to share. ~ Paul Zane Pilzer
- "Yesterday is gone. Tomorrow has not yet come. We have only today. Let us begin." ~ Mother Teresa

5. **SPIRITUAL OPTIMIZATION** – Taming of the Mind, Spirit before Ego - This connection provides awareness when we are able to put our spiritual path before our ego mind. This awareness is the sixth sense of seeing and thought management.

Quotes
- "The foundation of the Buddha's teachings lies in compassion, and the reason for practicing the teachings is to wipe out the persistence of ego, the number-one enemy of compassion."~ Tenzin Gyatso, the 14th Dalai Lama
- In the secret cave of the heart, two are seated by life's fountain. The separate ego drinks of the sweet and bitter stuff, Liking the sweet, disliking the bitter, While the supreme Self drinks sweet and bitter. Neither liking this nor disliking that. The ego gropes in darkness, while the Self lives in light. ~ Quote / Poem n° 3217 : Upanishads, Hinduism
- "Don't compare yourself with anyone in this world…if you do so, you are insulting yourself." — Bill Gates
- So Jesus said to them, "Truly, truly, I say to you, the Son can do nothing of his own accord, but only what he sees the Father doing. For whatever the Father does, that the Son does likewise. John 5:19

- Part of being a winner is knowing when enough is enough. Sometimes you have to give up the fight and walk away, and move on to something that's more productive. ~ Donald Trump

6. **POTENTIAL** - To maximize awake-ness, we must compartmentalize our day. Each day gives us new lessons and life's challenges. We learn and we grow. With contemplative action, we can enter the 4th dimension of living. We defragment our minds and souls through a practical, psychological clearing process. Using this process, we eliminate and mitigate non-productive thoughts. We must banish blame, put aside blocks to our happiness, learn to stop distractions, and begin to engage true focus on our growth and happiness. We begin to release instinctual judgments of people, places and things. This is where liberation begins & we enable our minds to see the beauty, awe, and beneficence of the universe.

Quotes

- The will to win, the desire to succeed, the urge to reach your full potential... these are the keys that will unlock the door to personal excellence. ~ Confucius
- Jesus: "Those who want to save their life will lose it, and those who lose their life for my sake will save it." Mark 8:35
- Buddha: "With the relinquishing of all thought and egotism, the enlightened one is liberated through not clinging." Majjhima Nikaya 72:15
- "Always dream and shoot higher than you know you can do. Do not bother just to be better than your contemporaries or predecessors. Try to be better than yourself." ~ William Faulkner
- "The starting point of all achievement is DESIRE. Keep this constantly in mind. Weak desire brings weak results, just as

a small fire makes a small amount of heat." — Napoleon Hill, Think and Grow Rich

7. **PURPOSE** – FOCUS, CONCENTRATION, MEANING - Transcend fear, scarcity, anger, frustration and lack. Abundance and faith is an inside job and esoteric procedure. By eliminating these blocks to the sunlight of the spirit, we approach unity with our spiritual self, which is connected to the force of the universe.

Quotes

- "He who has a why to live for can bear almost any how." ~ Friedrich Nietzsche
- "Your purpose in life is to find your purpose and give your whole heart and soul to it" ~ Gautama Buddha
- Our prime purpose in this life is to help others. And if you can't help them, at least don't hurt them. ~ Dalai Lama
- "The purpose of art is washing the dust of daily life off our souls". ~ Pablo Picasso
- Any idea, plan, or purpose may be placed in the mind through repetition of thought. ~ Napoleon Hill
- There is one quality which one must possess to win, and that is definiteness of purpose, the knowledge of what one wants, and a burning desire to possess it. ~ Napoleon Hill
- "We are products of our past, but we don't have to be prisoners of it."
  ~ Rick Warren, The Purpose Driven Life: What on Earth Am I Here for?
- Success is not final, failure is not fatal: it is the courage to continue that counts. ~ Winston Churchill

8. **HARMONY** – PEACE OF MIND, FORGIVENESS - We must cleanse our mind and senses by working through our past and developing harmonious thinking. We then can grow closer to peace of mind and our natural purpose. The goal is to unfold and become what we are meant to be. We are to fully express our life and potentiality.

Quotes
- Jesus said, *"And when you stand praying, if you hold anything against anyone, forgive him, so that your Father in heaven may forgive you your sins."* (Mark 11:25)
- "Peace comes from within. Do not seek it without." — Buddha
- "Nothing external to you has any power over you." — RW Emerson
- "Pleasure is always derived from something outside you, whereas joy arises from within." — Eckhart Tolle
- "The wise man does not lay up his own treasures. The more he gives to others, the more he has for his own." Lao Tzu
- 'He abused me, he struck me, he overcame me, he robbed me' – in those who do not harbor such thoughts hatred will cease. (Dhammapada 1.3-4; translation. w:Radhakrishnan).
- "Be kind and compassionate to one another, forgiving each other, just as in Christ God forgave you." (Ephesians 4:32)
- "When you hold resentment toward another, you are bound to that person or condition by an emotional link that is stronger than steel. Forgiveness is the only way to dissolve that link and get free." — Catherine Ponder
- If one who has been wronged by another does not wish to rebuke or speak to the offender – because the offender is simple or confused – then if he sincerely forgives him, neither bearing him ill-will nor administering a reprimand, he acts according to the standard of the pious. (Deot 6:9).

- "A big part of financial freedom is having your heart and mind free from worry about the what-ifs of life." — Suze Orman

9. **CREATIVITY** - Relationships must become harmonious and driven by harmlessness while being inspired by our spiritual giving selves. Generally, we are driven to be over-dependent, defiant, or rebellious toward others. Beginning anew, we can now operate from a spiritual, prosperous, clear and authentic place, we can transcend these instincts and respond in a spiritual way rather than react to others in relations.

Quotes

- Whatever you can do, or dream you can do, begin it. Boldness has genius, power, and magic in it. Begin it now to heat the mind and complete the tasks... ~ Goethe
- "It is better to live your own destiny imperfectly than to live an imitation of somebody else's life with perfection." ~ Anonymous, The Bhagavad Gita
- Whatever you do, work heartily, as for the Lord and not for men. Colossians 3:23
- Burning desire to be or do something gives us staying power - a reason to get up every morning or to pick ourselves up and start in again after a disappointment. Do what you love and the money will follow. ~ Marsha Sinetar
- "The painter has the Universe in his mind and hands." — Leonardo da Vinci
- "As my sufferings mounted I soon realized that there were two ways in which I could respond to my situation -- either to react with bitterness or seek to transform the suffering into a creative force. I decided to follow the latter course." — Martin Luther King Jr.

10. **VISUALIZATION –** With the development of our imagination, we learn to picture our goals and dreams in our mind. We further discover how to cultivate a feeling that "All is right with my World" Begin at home and learn to build relationships with complements, praise and support. Prayer and visualization and feeling are linked on a spiritual and universal level. An affirmation or prayer should be utilized in a way that invokes feeling and energy to the core of your spirit. This can be called cognitive cellular transformation CCT. Using prayer, visualization and affirmations must be optimized so that your consciousness is lifted up. If you must hit your knees or gently tap your chest while praying, these techniques can help infuse your spirit with a higher energy and higher connection with the spiritual source of all. Seeing the results of your visualization or affirmation in your mind's eye is part of the visualization process. Feeling what you see in your mind's eye is yet another step.

Quotes:
- Now faith is the assurance of things hoped for, the conviction of things not seen. For by it the people of old received their commendation. By faith we understand that the universe was created by the word of God, so that what is seen was not made out of things that are visible. Hebrews 11:1-3
- Jesus answered him, "Truly, truly, I say to you, unless one is born again he cannot see the kingdom of God." John 3:3
- "I learned this, at least, by my experiment: that if one advances confidently in the direction of his dreams, and endeavors to live the life which he has imagined, he will meet with a success unexpected in common hours." — Henry David Thoreau, Walden: Or, Life in the Woods

11. **CONTEMPLATION** - Prayer and Meditation - Seek inspiration and quiet time. Find the flow and connection to the Spirit of the Universe. Seek your authentic voice of ideas. Learn how to take affirmative action toward your dreams. Learn to speak your truth. Learn to pray for protection, and contemplate love, health and wealth. Develop a higher consciousness and connectedness. Contemplation is also key because it affords us time to develop receptivity. Receptivity means that we develop openness to the flow of ideas to us and allow ourselves to be perceptive enough to see signs in which to act upon.

Quotes:
- "When meditation is mastered, the mind is unwavering, like the flame of a lamp in a windless place." ~ **Krishna**
- "Meditation in its essence is the art of seeing into the nature of one's being, and it points the way from bondage to freedom." ~ **DT Suzuki**
- Right understanding, with true longing, absolute trust, and sweet grace-giving mindfulness ~ ***Julian of Norwich***
- The function of prayer is not to influence God, but rather to change the nature of the one who prays." — Søren Kierkegaard
- "If the only prayer you said was thank you, that would be enough." — Meister Eckhart
- The memory of God comes to the quiet mind. (ACIM p. 457)

12. **ONGOING INVENTORY** - We must limit our blocks to freedom as well as our character flaws. Continuously evaluate what works and what does not work. We must begin using what works each day based on the success of actions, inactions and thinking. Practice these steps so that you can optimize your knowingness of the Spirit of the Universe. Get and Stay lucid, release peace, radiate love.

Quotes:

- "He who knows others is wise; he who knows himself is enlightened." — Lao Tzu
- Therefore, confess your sins to one another and pray for one another, that you may be healed. The prayer of a righteous person has great power as it is working. James 5:16
- "No one is free who has not obtained the empire of himself. No man is free who cannot command himself." — Pythagoras
- 1 John 1:9 If we confess our sins, he is faithful and just to forgive us our sins and to cleanse us from all unrighteousness.
- James 5:16 Therefore, confess your sins to one another and pray for one another, that you may be healed. The prayer of a righteous person has great power as it is working.
- Proverbs 28:13 Whoever conceals his transgressions will not prosper, but he who confesses and forsakes them will obtain mercy.
- The weak can never forgive. Forgiveness is the attribute of the strong. Mahatma Gandhi
- Do not be conformed to this world, but be transformed by the renewal of your mind, that by testing you may discern what is the will of God, what is good and acceptable and perfect. ~ Romans 12:2

13. **CHARACTER** – Your Mind and Body is your temple – We must learn to feed our body and mind with only the things that will provide abundant and prosperous emotions and ideas. Learn from lessons and continue to maximize your potential. Our thinking is part of our character. We become what we think. Constructive thinking based in gratitude can allow us to see the best in life.

Quotes:

- Nearly all men can stand adversity, but if you want to test a man's character, give him power. Abraham Lincoln
- Character cannot be developed in ease and quiet. Only through experience of trial and suffering can the soul be strengthened, ambition inspired, and success achieved. Helen Keller
- Character is higher than intellect. A great soul will be strong to live as well as think. Ralph Waldo Emerson
- Our characters are the result of our conduct. Aristotle, Nicomachean Ethics (c. 335 B.C).
- Our character is the totality of our thinking, actions and inactions. Our goal is to develop the power to maximize our character. ~ Magus Incognito – Essays
- Only by strict specialization can the scientific worker become fully conscious, for once and perhaps never again in his lifetime, that he has achieved something that will endure. A really definitive and good accomplishment is today always a specialized act. ~ Max Weber
- *Es bildet ein Talent sich in der Stille, Sich ein Charakter in dem Strom der Welt.* "Talent is nurtured in solitude; character is formed in the stormy billows of the world." ~ Johann Wolfgang von Goethe, *Torquato Tasso*, I, 2, 66.

14. **LOVE** - When we are in flow, tuned in to our spiritual selves, we realize that GOD is LOVE. Love is patient, kind, unselfish, giving, generous, humble, understanding, thankful, grateful, compassionate, and more. Using these virtues is pure Wisdom. Become "in love" with your soul and the Spirit of the Universe. Miracles occur naturally as expressions of love. They are performed by those who temporarily have more for those who temporarily have less. (ACIM p. 1) Love dissipates resentments and affords forgiveness and clarity.

Quotes on Love
- "Your task is not to seek for love, but merely to seek and find all the barriers within yourself that you have built against it." Rumi
- You may receive love from many, but until you learn to give it & truly radiate love to others, you will not see the spark of life and joy that surrounds you. Magus Incognito
- Greater love hath no man than this, that a man lay down his life for his friends. Jesus Christ, in John 15:13
- "Since the only Presence and Power of the Universe loves me and sustains me, what on earth could I possibly fear? Nothing. No - thing. Love heals, love prospers, love protects, love gaurds, love guides, love restores, love creates, love makes all things new. So I let love go before me now to straighten out every crooked place in my life. I place my faith in God's love for me, and I am free, as I was created to be." John Randolph Price from "The Love Book"
- TO LOVE is to find pleasure in the happiness of others. Gottfried Leibniz, A Dialogue (c. 1696).
- Perfect love casts out fear. If fear exists, then there is not perfect love. (p.12)
- Love our neighbors as ourselves. Jesus Christ, *Gospels of Mark, Matthew and John*
- The true Yogi applies the same standard to others as he applies to himself. Seeing what is pleasure and pain for himself, he

knows what is pleasure and pain for others. Thus, he wishes good to all and evil to none.
The Bagavad Gita
- If we sacrifice this body for the world's benefit, the all things will come to that person who loves others as he loves himself.
The Tao Te Ching
- Being immersed in the highest state of consciousness, the disciple's heart is connected to compassion. He sees himself in all beings, and is free from negative feelings toward others.
Doctrinal Formulas

15. **KNOWING** - Be open to the power, healing and perfection of divine power and flow. When you have the knowingness and beingness, you are, in fact, filled with the holy spirit of the universe. You will then live in a higher order of being in the 4th dimension.

Quotes:

- All who call on God in true faith, earnestly from the heart, will certainly be heard, and will receive what they have asked and desired. **Martin Luther**
- As for God, "I don't need to believe, I Know" – **Dr. Carl Jung**
- Develop an attitude of gratitude, and give thanks for everything that happens to you, knowing that every step forward is a step toward achieving something bigger and better than your current situation. ~ Brian Tracy
- The unwise man is awake all night worries over and again. When morning rises
he is restless still, his burden as before. ~ The Havamal
- "Your beliefs become your thoughts, Your thoughts become your words, Your words become your actions, Your actions

become your habits, Your habits become your values, Your values become your destiny." — Mahatma Gandhi

- "All I have seen teaches me to trust the Creator for all I have not seen." — Ralph Waldo Emerson
- According to the Gospels, a Roman centurion asked Jesus for help because his boy servant was ill. Jesus offered to go to the centurion's house to perform the healing, but the centurion said, ""Lord, I do not deserve to have you come under my roof. But just say the word, and my servant will be healed." When Jesus heard this, he said to the people about the Roman Warrior: "Truly I tell you, I have not found anyone in Israel with such great faith."

The Use of Imagination for Powerful Intuition

By: G Mentz, Esq.

This is a discussion of the imagination with a focus on the teachings of various self help legends such as: Ben Franklin, Marcus Aurelius, Sun Tzu, Emerson, Thoreau, Napoleon Hill, Thomas Troward, James Allen, Wallace Wattles, Norman Vincent Peale, Neville Goddard, and Charles Haanel.

The world is but a canvas to the imagination. ~ HENRY DAVID THOREAU

In the following steps, the beauty and power of the imagination is illuminated. The secrets of how to use imagination as a force for creation and greatness are shown below. Enjoy.

1. We must learn to imagine ourselves in the right state of consciousness, and we must present ideas to our deeper mind and allow our consciousness to accept the ideas.
2. We must learn to think and view the world from a state of consciousness.
3. We must begin to learn how to think from the "finish line", think from the result, or think in the essence of victory
4. Learn to think from a state of mind or a mindset of having and enjoying something

5. We must learn to be in the assumption of having and be able see and feel ourselves "as if" the thing has happened. Think "from" the destiny.

6. In many cases we can think about a desired result or an answer to a question and look at all of the things that would be true for that result to happen.

7. Imagine looking at a matrix or a mosaic of successful outcomes that would need to happen for the ideal or desire to be manifested.

8. Remember that determined imagination or thinking from the "endgame or result" is the beginning of all great manifestation.

Imagination is the true magic carpet. ~ NORMAN VINCENT PEALE

9. We must imagine ourselves in the feeling of the result fulfilled during our waking hours and before bedtime.

10. We must create a dominant stream of thoughts which would be necessary to be that thing, be the energy of the desire, or to have that thing.

11. This quality of imagination would give us the state of mind or the superior mindset of being into with the purpose or the desired result

12. We can translate imagination and vision into being and becoming.

13. Thinking from the place of purpose is an intense perception of the world of fulfilled desire.

14. Thinking from a standpoint of the desired outcome is creative living.

15. We must put the past into our history and allow our present thoughts to manifest a state of mind which have become a future reality.

16. We have a purpose or find a purpose or seek a purpose we begin to cultivate the necessary hunger in relation to that purpose. That hunger will help continually cultivate the dominant thoughts and the state of mind and the mindset necessary to manifest a greater imagination and results.

17. An imagination is not just limited to the senses of taste, feel, smell, sound or site. Imagination is something where you can close your eyes and see something that you would enjoy in your life and look at it and see the essence of it.

"Imagination should be used, not to escape reality, but to create it." ~ Colin Wilson

18. For example, if you wanted to be a professional tennis player or a professional pianist, you would see the essence of that result, see yourself performing with crowds, see yourself winning championships, seeing yourself making execution of points or the excellent execution of musical abilities. Seeing yourself victoriously being paid, the type of compensation that is required for a professional.

19. At some point, you will be able to master a state of consciousness where your dominant thoughts generally pertain towards the results that you desire.

Those dominant thoughts would focus on sending you toward the direction of your goals.

20. This brings us to the idea that your dominant thoughts basically consist of your inner self talk and how you talk to yourself, and the visions, the patterns of the ideas that you see flowing through your consciousness.

21. If you can seize control over your mind and your memory and directed in a constructive way towards what you want, then you have effectively seized control of your dominant thinking.

Everything you can imagine is real.~ PABLO PICASSO

22. The real key is to align your mind and your memory and align your inner character and your goals with each other.

23. Accordingly, when great people say you have to "become that thing" that you want, that means aligning your energy, aligning your vibration, aligning your thinking, & aligning your skills in your mind with that result that you seek.

24. As such, when the inner and outer worlds match each other is how reality is created.

25. Some teachers talk about using a trance state or a hypnotic state to push imagination and ideas into the deeper consciousness. The ancient shamans called it Utiseta or "sitting out" which is an exercise where you are able to be in a " clear and peaceful

state of mind" with no distractions and you are able to concentrate your mind on things that you want so as to use your imagination in a very vital and constructive way.

26. When your imagination is so vivid and vital that it becomes real to you. You could sense it. You could touch it. You can do exercises with yourself where you see yourself in a particular situation where you can physically and mentally and emotionally feel the joy of that thing or that essence of being who you want to become. The idea is using your imagination to be, do and have what you want.

"Live out of your imagination, not your history." ~ Stephen R. Covey

27. Generally some experts talk about how you must become fascinated or intrigued with what you really want. Using your imagination to see and feel happy about something you love. Something that you want to become dedicated and committed to.

28. It's something that you think about happily and you look forward to. It is the harmonious and positive imagination regarding "what you want" that binds you to it. It creates a pleasant binding effect every time you imagine something with positive feeling,

29. You are binding, imagining and aligning yourself with what you desire.

30. The key with aligning yourself is so that your mind is not divided. They always say you don't want a divided house. Similarly, we don't want a divided

mind neither. You want your mind, both sides of your mind and your heart and your soul cooperating with each other.

31. To unify your mental house, sometimes that requires you to weed out the garden as they say and remove some of the anger or the resentment or the prideful emotions that you may have that are connected to something and allow those things to be purged and let go of your mind.

32. You purify yourself so you can have a more clear and emptier space in your heart in your mind to allow for your imagination to grow effectively and to become aligned with who and what you want to be and what you want to have be and do.

33. While all desires and results require action, the action begins in your mind and your imagination. There are many great Olympic sportsman or warriors with the military who rehearse every particular event in their mission plans and make sure they understand each task or point from beginning to end. They rehearse what needs to be done in their imagination. Also with this mental and physical practice, it helps winners get in the mindset of being aligned with and receptive to what they want to have.

"The best use of imagination is creativity." ~ Deepak Chopra

34. You have to center your imagination in the fulfilled desire with complete awareness and sensitiveness. This imagination can initiate optimal rewiring of neural pathways of your inner world.

35. Sometimes to begin something new and to begin something great, we must allow the old self to die out. The old personality or the old habits can be put aside so we can change our worldview, change our attitudes, change our habits, and change our heart.

36. We can become a new and open person where we can allow our deeper selves to have what we really, really want.

37. Sometimes this may require us to rewrite or overwrite the past and sometimes it may require us to review our mindset and look at our memory of certain events and purge them.

38. If it is something that you feel that you were wronged or something that you feel angry resentful about, sometimes you may be required to take that situation and look at it for what you learned about life or what lessons you learned from that situation

39. Even in bad experience, every time something has happened negative in our life, there is a seed of power victory. There is a seed of lessons in that we never have to repeat those particular situations again, can avoid problem, and overcome obstacles that most people can't deal with.

40. To become renewed and seek new greatness, there will be time where we have to allow ourselves to release old anger, destructive habits, or release

resentment because we want to be able to purge the mental garbage.

41. If we can't forgive, we may need to just let the rubbish go so we can move on.

The man who has no imagination has no wings. ~ MUHAMMAD ALI

42. We do not want to waste time and be at war with ourselves and nobody wants unnecessarily relive past events in our minds.

43. We need to remember that the quality of our "frame of mind" and the purity of your mindset is extremely important.

44. Achieving optimal mind sometimes requires us to forgive and forget but mainly to quit wasting time harping on things, to quit revisiting events in our mind.

45. Sometimes it's easier to fill the mind rather than just empty it. I remember a great class many years ago where a teach had dirty water in a glass bowl. He then took a hose and started pouring clean water into the dirty bowl of water and it was overflowing at the top. After about five minutes the water was clear in the bowl.

46. So the point is, is there is two ways to renew and cleanse the consciousness. There is <u>emptying</u> and then there is <u>filling</u>. The key to this exercise is that filling yourself with things that are exciting makes you feel alive and filling your mind with ideas and events

you are interested in and are fascinated with changes our attitudes and beliefs.

47. By that active filling you are releasing and purging, overwriting and pushing out the types of messages and patterns and habits of thinking that are not useful to you.

48. The Key point here is working to control your dominant self talk. If you increase dominant self talk in a certain area that are constructive and positive and uplifting, at some point your mind or your mindset or your vibration will become persuaded. It will be changed. It will be improved but it will be persuaded with new types of beliefs that will have overwritten the mental state or even the neurons that fire in your brain. They will fire differently after they are trained to fire in certain ways with regard to what you are more interested in and what you are you are more passionate about.

"The possible's slow fuse is lit by the imagination." ~ Emily Dickinson

49. Over time your inner speech, that dominant speech, that pattern over time will be like a new weaving a certain type of threads into a garment. Over time the garment becomes what you are thinking about. More and more over time, the garment looks like the new types of thoughts and the types of habits and thinking that you have woven into the fabric of your life.

50. So again in your thinking, we need to observe our inner speech, observe our dominant thoughts and observe those patterns. Because the thoughts that we have, if we pick certain thoughts and certain symbols and certain images in our imagination, we begin to attach certain symbols and certain words and certain ideas to what we want.

51. So we are attaching our inner ideas and binding them towards our vision and our purpose to augment our worldview and our awareness is what it does.

52. Remember many times when you change your worldview or you change your attitudes, you expand your awareness in the process. So let's just say for instance you have a new idea and your new idea is to get a certain type of clothing or a certain type of car, or golf clubs. Your awareness of those new ideas and things becomes heightened. Your awareness of the ideas or dreams that you desire to accomplish is clearer and the path become more reasonable.

53. When you focus on something, even your awareness of the actual thing becomes heightened. Everybody knows if you buy a certain computer or a certain phone or a certain car, as soon as you have that thing you actually will start noticing others who actually have that type of car. More often you will see that type of car on the street. You will notice your awareness is much higher because you know what that thing is. You understand what that thing is.

"I found I could say things with color and shapes that I couldn't say any other way–things I had no words for." - Georgia O'Keefe, Painter

54. That's one of the keys with imagination and dominant thoughts along with inner speech. The secret is whatever it is that you want to become, you start to know what that is. You study it, you know what it is on the inside and the outside. You know what the essence or benefits of that thing is. You know what it does. You know how it works. You know the actual dynamics or specs of that thing. That's why again they say to receive something you have to become it or become in alignment with it or match it in energy.

55. When you know what something is, you recognize it easier. In actuality your mindset needs to be of a harmonious mindset because only those that are harmonious find harmony and they never have to seek for it.

56. The people that become harmonious attract harmony.

57. This is just another reason why over the last hundred years, affirmations have become so popular. Prayers and petitions over the last 3000 years have been very popular. Mantras, spiritual poetry, prayers, psalms or repetitious types of readings where you either read or chant something out loud or in silence have been used for millennia .

58. All these practices of speaking and praying your petitions or incantations are said to help change your mindset, to help change your worldview and it also change your vibration in the way you see things.

59. It can be said that speech is the objectification of the images and the symbols and actions or the reverse of that is images and symbols and actions actually can become your inner speech. They are intertwined backwards and forwards.

"The future belongs to those who believe in the beauty of their dreams." -Eleanor Roosevelt, Politician

60. Remember we need to find our chief aim and purpose. We need to find that desire or goal that we really want and can easily persuade ourselves to accept. Something that we can believe that we are worthy of, something that we can see as our potentiality.

61. Then we need to align with it in both action and speech. Align with our desire, align with our purpose. The right to inner speech is essential.

62. Even if you think about the ancient teachings from the East where they talk about virtuous: speech and mind and awareness. Right speech. Right mind. Right awareness.

63. If you confuse your inner talk in your mind with your outer talk there will be conflict. We need to bring them in alignment with each other and then your actions, tasks, and abilities will manifest much more quickly toward our potential.

64. Generally speaking we are in control of our thought and we are the cause of our inner mental discussion.

65. Now if we seek inspiration, that is a different process of seeking ideas and a stream of thought from the Universe, but your typical daily self talk is another thing. If you activate your inner receptivity, innovative thoughts can come from the universe. Like Edison and Einstein, both would take naps or rest to seek out solutions to problems.

66. So alignment is key but what is also vital is cultivating gratitude and feeling. It is powerful to feel grateful for what is going on in your life now. Becoming thankful for your actions and your thinking now.

67. Choose positive thoughts in relation to what you want.

68. We have to assume the essence of being what we want to be. I mentioned that once before and I will mention it again that we have to assume the essence. Here is an example of Essence: So if you want to complete a marathon, you have to see yourself going through it. See yourself going through every part of that race with all the different turns and twists and knowing how much time there will be left at a certain point. Then at the end of the marathon, see yourself completing it and finishing the achievement in a healthy and happy way is your ESSENCE.

69. You can learn to pre-feel the "essence of being" a winner and essence of being a finisher of that particular event for example.

70. Review and remember your actions. Reflect in your imagination on what you have done well each day and things you may not have excelled upon. Be determined to be better and do the right thing. Over

200 years ago, Ben Franklin worked his "precepts of order" each evening. He wanted to be excellent and build his character even at a mature age. Practice imagining yourself doing something with excellence and being your best to your loved ones, in your work, or even imagine excellence with your creative or competitive future events.

71. Considering all of this, every thought that we have, every action that we have, every omission that we have, those things we have in the now are creating our now-ness but they are also weaving our future.

72. Create your inner speech in a way that blesses your life and others. Your inner speech should bless your health, happiness, love and prosperity.

Perhaps the real trouble was our almost total inability to point imagination toward the right objectives. Twelve Steps and Twelve Traditions, Bill W., Step Eleven, p.100

73. This may sound oversimplified but we have to make our inner speech blessed and create a flow of good information and good reports. By choosing good things to focus on, this focus forms and inner sense of gratitude, of grateful sense of self talk.

74. Thus, a Habitual or Habit of consciousness directed upon what we want with a vivid imagination pertaining to it, this clarifies and codifies our energy to manifest our desires.

75. So with each goal we have a choice and when we make that choice we have to decide whether or not we are going to accept it. When we accept something, it can become a belief or an assumed future belief.

76. So we are at a point where we are learning to fill ourselves, fill our hearts with the correct information, vibrations, and energy. Fill our minds with dominant ideas and dominant thoughts and dominant speech or inner self talk related to harmony, quality of life that we want.

77. We need to allow the excellent seed to flourish in our mental garden, and allow the bad seed of the garden really to wither, to be "pushed out" or to die out on its own. All of the unneeded ideas can be overcome with new and powerful ideas that are so strong that the constructive thought will push out from your mind what it is that is holding you back.

78. In the end, we learn to accomplish these exercises of mind and memory, self talk, and actions/omissions. When all of these things become aligned with each other towards the goals that we want to achieve success can blossom. Our alignment will be towards the happiness we want our lives, towards the health we want in our lives.

79. Most importantly, we need to identify with the new consciousness. We need to identify with that gratifying consciousness of what we want to be.

80. So you have to identify with the consciousness of prosperity, love, and harmony. Identify with the consciousness of health. Identify with the consciousness of wealth. All of these things are your consciousness including happiness, health, wealth,

worthiness, peace of mind, love. All of these qualities are the most important attributes for bliss and a magnificent recipe for success.

81. Remember you have to give yourself consent to allow a new mindset to build within your subconscious mind.

82. I think that's one of the most challenging things about changing attitudes, changing mindset, changing the way we act is one obstacle. This one obstacle is putting aside wishful-hope and allowing for ourselves to actually and finally change our deeply held beliefs.

83. We have to give ourselves consent, a mental consent and accept aspiration and authentic change.

"Anything you may hold firmly in your imagination can be yours." "Our view of the world is truly shaped by what we decide to hear." ~ William James "Father of American Psychology"

84. I truly believe that all of these concepts herein form the basis of "liberation spirituality" because you don't have to depend on anybody else for anything. When you become in alignment with yourself and the universe, people, places and things will begin to act in accordance with your harmonious goals. Goals that don't hurt anybody but goals that would help you and other people. Help you serve humanity in a greater way. This is what I mean by liberation spirituality. Each individual could become a greater person and exercise their talents and serve humanity with helping others with the solutions they may need in their life or

becoming the best you can be on a competitive level too.

85. So to rehash, it is important to learn how to shut out all non productive ideas and divisive seeds in our minds. Shut those things out that interfere with our vision and our purpose and our goals.

86. Learn to adjust our beliefs and put them at the forefront of our thinking in alignment with our desires and our purpose so as to activate the manifestation of the results what we seek.

87. To do these things we would fuse ourselves with our purpose and become at one with our purpose. Just like an actor gets into the role and mind of the character.

88. You could have many purposes. You should make yourself strong and great first for the benefit of yourself and all loved ones.

89. Your purpose may be helping other people find their path. It could be helping someone become physically healthy. It could be helping someone learn something because you are a teacher or an instructor. It could be any one of those things.

Active imagination requires a state of reverie, half-way between sleep and waking. Without this playing with fantasy no creative work has ever yet come to birth. The debt we owe to the play of the imagination is incalculable. ~ Carl Jung - "Father of Modern Analytical Psychology"

90. So we have to learn how to choose our state of being, choose our state of consciousness and imagine the receipt of your GOOD on a daily basis. Imagine ourselves in receipt of the essence and benefits of our desires. We have to learn to think from that place of joy and aliveness. Thing from the standpoint of having what we desire. Think from a place of what we will be able to be, have or do. It is only the ideals from which you think that our lives are realized. Your thought creates opportunity, a mindset, and a consciousness.

91. In this new consciousness, you will have heightened abilities of: awareness, mindfulness, productivity, effectiveness, thought, speech and clarity.

92. If you are having trouble at any time changing your mindset or breaking out of a mindset that you are stuck in, you need to find a thought or memory that you have that brightened your mood. Something from the past that you can latch onto mentally. Your victorious scene or your "peaceful scene" or your "successful scene" that you can picture in your imagination. You can train yourself to go back to that scene and imagine it "at will", and that will give you peace. With that piece of mind you are able to refocus and re-concentrate and what it is you want.

Conclusion

Remember this isn't about having perfect consciousness or having a perfect mindset that is directed towards your goal. It's really about getting your mindset over 50% clear and productive. Once you have a PMV positive mental vibration of over 50% most all of the time, you will be ahead of the vast majority of all people. You can now have a clear mental vibration of success, health, wealth, wholeness, worthiness, receptiveness, and aliveness. Once you allow yourself to get above 50%, the rewired consciousness takes over. The constructive mindset takes over as 51% of anything is greater than the rest and will color all else in it's vicinity. It's a majority and it takes over the entire mindset and that's the key.

Intuition Exercises and Prescience Techniques

Magical Guided Meditation – Consulting Your Holy Self

Step 1 - Before you go into any guided meditation, you should relax the body top to bottom and go into the alpha state which is the condition of a Relaxed Mind and Body. Focus your relaxation on each part of the body. Start with your toes and go all the way up through your legs and to your knees and hips and into your body. And take a deep breath and into your lungs and feel your heart beating and let it go all the way to the tips of your fingers and the tips of your toes and allow your body to relax. And all the way to the top of your head, to your mind and your eyes, and then to your crown, and just connect yourself all there is. That's the first step.

To be in a relaxed position, you can be sitting in a chair or lying down, which are probably the best two positions. It is probably not a good idea to do this while in the car, while I do believe that some of the advanced souls can be driving and do these exercises without a problem.

For beginners, it's best to do it in a quiet spot where you're not distracted. This as a directed exercise, you imagine yourself as your favorite animal for instance. It could be a lion, a falcon, an eagle, a tiger or bear, or it could be your favorite dog or cat. Imagine yourself as that animal traveling through the tranquil forest, or flying over a peaceful forest or lake. As you see a large fortress or castle, you enter into that sacred space. As you approach the fortress or the castle the doors open for you. You arrive there as the animal you are, and then you transform back into your warrior self.

Imagine a medieval castle and imagine your clothes being medieval armor and you walk into the castle, and as you walk into the great hall there is someone there at the end of the hall on a throne, and you walk up to that throne, and as you look at the person who is up there, you have a great realization. IT is in fact you, and you decide to have a conversation with your holy, royal self. And you ask questions, questions you've always wanted to ask yourself about what you should do, where you should travel one day. You can ask anything such as, what type of life you should have or what type of purpose you should live. What type of mission you should have in your life. What type of things you should create, what types of things you should go for. Whatever it might be, and this holy self will have a voice. A voice similar to yours, but it is NOT yours. It is a different but Authentic voice that is connected to the source of all good. It is the voice that can guide you, and give you peace, and give you direction, and when you finish discussing these things with your holy self. Thank your Holy Self. You can give the person a name if you want. It can be a man or a woman, even if it's not you, it can be someone of a different gender and still be you. But it represents you, and you thank your higher self for all the help and as you walk away, you close the door behind you knowing you can return at anytime.

You transform back into that part of your soul that is a mighty being or peaceful animal, and you come back to your home and body where you are in your imagination. In most cases you would open your eyes and you'd be back of course in your own reality. And you could take out a pen and paper and write notes, think about the experience, and then maybe try it again sometime soon. I want to encourage everybody to do this but keep in mind that you want to make sure that when you are traveling to this special place that it's at a peaceful time, that it's a peaceful journey, and take a few deep breaths and as you travel to this sacred shrine to visit your Holy Self, whether it be a castle or a fortress or anywhere, you want to make sure that your journey there is peaceful and serene, and that when you arrive there you are ready to have a meaningful discussion.

And that's about it for this particular exercise, and please remember that all exercises should be done in a safe place while not driving or operating machinery.

Exercises for Concentration, Intuition, Meditation, and Energy

Concentration Exercise

1. Find a relaxed part of your home
2. Sit and quiet the mind and begin to relax each part of the body (that you can think of) from head to toes.
3. Shut your eyes & take a few deep breaths.
4. Think of a room that you lived in as a child or that you are presently in.
5. Begin to see and visualized in your mind the entire room and its contents and where things are located. (Whatever you can recall)
6. It is also good to imagine the exact color of things in the room with your eyes closed.
7. This is also a good exercise to do even after you have entered a new building or place.
8. Do this for a few minutes each day and your focus and concentration will increase. These days, there is computer software that actually runs programs to help concentration in this same way..
9. As a note, this same type of exercise is also very good to relax and vividly recall wonderful people or possessions that you have in your past or present.

- Open your eyes when done with any of these exercises ☺

Active Meditation Exercise

1. Engage steps 1, 2 & 3 above.
2. With eyes closed and imagining, see yourself going into a sacred castle.
3. As you enter the main chamber, you see the (helpful person of your choice).
4. This person could be alive or from the past.
5. You then discuss with her or him in your minds eye. [imagination]
6. You ask questions and your Friendly Guru answers these questions.
7. Try and sense the answers from your core (heart and stomach).
8. When you are finished, thank your friend for the help and guidance.
9. You may have an overwhelming sense that this voice or person is from a higher or different viewpoint than your own.

Exercise for Energizing or Healing Yourself.

1) Engage steps 1,2, and 3 above. (Relaxing in a chair with spine straight) relax your hands on your lap.
2) Close your eyes and visualize a peaceful lake that has no ripples. Then see yourself surrounded by bright white particles of energy that also permeates your body.
3) In your mind, see the bright light move toward and focus on the area of discomfort or pain. Allow this white light to fill any affected area and flow thought your body.
4) Know that the white light brings all of your body's healing power to work most effectively for you.
5) Take a few breaths.
6) Then, allow this bright light to act like water and flow though your body.
7) Allow the "fluid of light" purify and wash your entire body.
8) Feel and see in your minds eye that the washing fluid of white light is "pure love" and cleanses you of ANY AND ALL fear, resentment, hurt, and dis-ease.
9) Say to yourself, I forgive myself and everyone for the past.

    Thank the light of the universe for removing any impurities from your body.
10) Claim mental freedom from all problems in your mind and spirit. Thank the universe for your health and peace.
11) See others in your mind's eye walking up to you and congratulating you on your healing and success.
12) That's it..... & Open your eyes.

Perception and Awareness Exercise

1. Sit is a relaxed position
2. Relax each part of the body and take a few deep breaths.
3. Imagine a warm energy radiating through your body.
4. Enter what we call the Alpha State – which is Relaxed Daydreaming and Right Brain.
5. Now, begin to feel or sense each part of the body.
6. Direct your attention to your toes or hands or ears.
7. Notice how each part of the body feels.
8. Now close your eyes and notice any sounds either of your body or around you.
9. See if you can hear something far away.
10. Now, refocus and imagine just one sound or image.
11. Focus all of your thought on seeing, hearing, feeling, or tasting/smelling only one thing that you imagine.
12. Imagine this one thing to the exclusion of everything else.
13. As an example, try to imagine just the sound of a soft trumpet or French horn playing a song.
14. After a few minutes, relax again and come back to your BETA state of mind and consciousness. Left Brain

Affirmation Exercises

1. Affirmations should be affirmative. Each affirmation can be written in an "AS IF" phrase or sentence.

2. Affirmations can be for health, success, peace, safety, relationships, or even supply in the form of money.

3. Affirmations can be said out loud or in silence. Some people love to do their affirmations in the mirror.

4. A prime example of an affirmation could be, " I am healthy, happy, successfully, loved and whole. I am part Supreme Intelligence and the Supreme only creates beauty and perfection."

5. Keep in mind, you should have an "essence in back of affirmations". As an example, a supply affirmation could say, "I will earn an extra 5000 dollars in the next 4 weeks by providing excellent service as a salesperson or expert or by effectively serving others...."

6. As you can see, the above affirmation specifies some distinct creative work and cooperation related to your prosperity, and it is not a blind or hopeful demand to receive something for nothing. You can always affirm mentally or out loud for possibilities and opportunities.

7. There are primary reasons against blind affirmations for things or money of which we will not discuss at length. However, if a person demands 100 thousand dollars from the

supreme, it may come in the form of an injury settlement which might not be your first choice.

8. Overall, we should state our affirmations with confidence, love, harmony, gratitude, and faith. With this combination, the universe will gladly begin working to unfold opportunities and blessings for you.

9. As such, a clear thought or idea that is repeated again and again is almost certain to manifest a replica of itself in the future. If the thought is held strongly, with gratitude and feeling, and in a creative way that does not hurt others, your desire will come quickly as the imagined formulation or something even better will unfold.

Prescience and Intuition

This section is about how to develop your intuition or our inspiration. First of all, what's the difference between inspiration and intuition? Well, let's say you start your morning with some meditation. You sit down and you read some meditative books. And, you ponder them and you muse over those ideas that you've read, that information that you've read. And, as you sit peacefully with your quiet mind, while ideas begin to flow to you about what you should do with your day, or some other concern in relation to the reading that you've had.

And, from those ideas you've received some inspiration which technically is a type of intuition. And, this information has come to you, and you need to decide how to act upon it. And, the best way to decide upon any intuition or any inspiration that you've received, an idea from the universe is to filter it through some simple ethical and virtuous principles such as: lovingness, and kindness, and is it pure and good for your mind, is it harmless to other people, is it good for you and other people, is it unselfish and is it loving. Those are just some basic principles that you should use.

Furthermore, the ideas should be backed by some facts so that the idea is a calculated risk but probable success. Thus, if the facts back up your idea, if you act upon the idea with action, belief, intent, planning, and hard work, the probability of success is good.

10 Exercises and Practices of Seeking Intuition, Prescience and Inspiration of Consciousness.

1) *Talk to Your Higher Self Exercise*

One, you might want to go through a guided meditation or guided fantasy of sorts. You can imagine yourself going to a beautiful castle in the mountains, and you arrive there, and you walk into the hall of a beautiful castle room, and you see someone at the throne there, and low and behold, it's you. It's you, but it's the glorified, the wonderful you who's the king or queen of the castle. And, you go and speak directly to that person. You sit down next to them or in front of them or stand in front of them, and you ask questions. And, once you ask a question in your mind's eye, you wait for the answer and see what comes.

The magic of this mindful practice is that for many people another genuine tone of voice will RESPOND. It's an authentic voice different from yours, and it will give answers to your questions. Like should I take this job, or should I invest in this certain venture, should I be better friends with a certain person, or take the relationship to another level. These are just some basic examples. Or, should I move to a different place, or foreign land, etc.. The goal here is to make friends with your Higher Self and learn to seek the wisdom to the deeper and authentic self which knows your truth and the best answers for you.

2) Magic Door Exercise

The second practice or exercise is you go to the same castle in your mind where you go to a special room with a door. Then, you ask a question to yourself before you go to the door, and when the door opens, after you've asked the question, there's either going to be a yes or no in your mind when the door opens.

3) Divining Symbols

The third way might be to use a card or a rune or some type of decision piece, and you ask a question and you pick one of the cards or the runes or the decision piece, and it can give you an answer, a yes or a no, or maybe, or descriptive words ideas or symbols. There're various different types of decision type cards or runes, and each card might have a different response or a different opinion on it about what to do. That's just one example, or you can use an object to help you with your intuition.

4) Contemplative Object

The fourth practice is contemplative intuitive practice. This exercise would be to pick an object, maybe it could be a stain glass window or a beautiful picture. And, you focus on it for a while. The object could be a crystal or special rock. And, you observe it, and you look deeply at it, and you become receptive, and perceptive. And, you allow the feelings to come into you, and you allow the impressions and inspiration and ideas and intuition to flow to you. Doing this, you're somewhat in a trance state focusing on a particular object and nothing else, focusing on one object while avoiding all other things around you without distraction. And, that's the type of deep contemplation somewhat akin to Taizé meditation of the mystical Catholics. Almost all cultures have some type of iconic meditative practice.

5) Meditative Musing

And, number five would be just to read an affirmation or meditation and then to have some quiet time, and to allow thoughts and ideas and inspiration to come to you. I mentioned this before, but it could be a meditative book, or many people in different literatures have suggested that you just open a page in your favorite wisdom literature. It could be the Bible, Old Testament or New Testament. It could be some Native American, Vedic or Buddhist writings. It doesn't matter. And, you just open a page to it, you read it, and then meditate over that, and you allow, without distraction for your quiet time. To begin, it is sometimes best to take a few deep breaths, relaxed your body from head to toe, and you're able to go through this process of just allowing your mind to receive this beautiful information that comes from in and around the universe. With this practice you may have some aha moments from time to time which resolve long standing questions or challenges.

6) Look for Signs based on a Question

Number six, you can ask a question in the morning or in the evening, it doesn't matter. Let's say you ask a question in the morning of yourself like would it be good for me to move to Washington D.C., or London, it doesn't matter.

And, you ask that question very quietly and very assertively to yourself in the morning in a relaxed way. And during that day, you look for signs. You look for signs and symbols from the universe that may guide you. And, let's say you're driving down the road that day, and you see a sign that says Washington or London or whatever it might be. Let's say that somebody starts talking about they had a great time while living at a certain place and you learn more. That's just an example of how you could ask a question and look for signs in your daily life.

7)   Pattern Writing

And number seven, you write out ideas or questions that come to you mind and you keep writing them out on a scrap of paper. Let's say you write out, should I take this job, or should I move to this place, or should I invest in this investment, and you write these things down, you just keep writing out what comes to your mind. It could be anything. And, as you write these things out, maybe you'll see a **<u>pattern</u>** in the writing. And, that pattern on that page may, the totality of the ideas may give you sign or a symbol or some path to take, or some way to act or not act. This may be especially effective with the type of work or hobbies that you seek. The overall pattern of ideas may point you to a type of work that you may master and become great at doing.

8) *Imagine Decisions in the Future*

Another way to imagine doing something, a decision, imagine taking action in your life in some area, and then lock that idea in mentally and basically bring it down from your mind into your heart, almost like swallowing it, and feel this decision's impact on you and try to feel it in your heart, mind, and gut, but particularly in your gut.

So, you are imagine doing something like buying a house or a condo or a car, or moving to another place, or taking a job. You are imagining a new future event, you are imagining what it's like, imagining the outcome, and then you try to feel in your gut whether or not it is good or bad. Is it a yes or a no feeling?

And then you mentally turn on the computer in your mind and select the future time and date and result to see if the decision is beneficial or prevents harm, where it is not harmful. So, the key to this is really locking in some moment in the future, maybe a year from now, whatever, and just imagining what that future experience is like. It's got to be a little bit specific, but other than that, it's a good way to formulate the potentiality of a a yes or no feeling in your center of emotions and gut.

9) *Object Holding Exercise – Sense the Energy*

Another quick exercise would be maybe to hold an object that represents what the future might be and try and see if your imagination presents any ideas or events based on holding that object, whether you receive a little mental-movie clip or an idea that's running through your mind.

This is yet another simple exercise to test your intuition or your inspiration.

10) *The Papal Bowl of Intuition Exercise*

Another exercise would be to cut out a couple of slips of paper and write on each slip of paper a particular action that you might take, or an object that you want or a type of car, it doesn't matter, and you are just writing three or four ideas on pieces of paper. You are sticking them in a bowl and you allow maybe one of your children to pick something from the bowl or a trusted friend. This is an idea that's been around forever. Even some of the popes in foreign lands are picked this way. In Egypt, the pope is selected by, they put three names of three Bishops in a bowl, and they allow a small child to pick one of the names out of the bowl and that's how the Pope is selected in the Coptic Church in Egypt.

In sum, this is a very existential practice of knowing yourself and trying to be your best and basically existentialism is really the freedom that lies where your authentic self is discovered.

11) Bonus Technique

Simply ask or pose a question. You can write it down if you like. Example: Should I call a certain friend or partner business partner. Then, open any book with your eyes closed and pick a page and point to a part of the page. Open your eyes and analyze the words near your finger. Do these words give you inspiration or an answer? If not, there is no need to act, but there may be signs within the descriptive words and ideas that you have picked.

In The Moment Intuition – Power of Inspiration

Wealth is a force for good, a force for learning, helps create experiences, funds expanded talents, and allows for expanded giving. In the essence of wealth, our reality is our acceptance of good. Success and prosperity and financial freedom is a reasonable option in life. Therefore, accepting the reasonableness and possibility of good in every moment is a present form or wealth consciousness.

Exercises to Harness Your Passions in Life

1. Take a moment to list the ideas that you have in the moment right now, and meditate on your objectives that you have. And then, listen to yourself and see what your thoughts are around your goals and objectives.

2. And then, mentally engage your idea, and then you can build upon the idea with action and allow innovation and improvisation.

3. What decision feels right? Use your gut without focusing on limited data. Change routines or do something differently, and empty yourself of your preconceptions.

4. What makes you feel alive? What is your passion? What would you do for free if you could do it?

5. How can you serve that will help the most people?

6. Earnestly commit to a full, free, and spiritual, and wealthy life.

7. Be good to yourself and know yourself and let go of your blocks and mental hindrances to your happiness.

8. Decide to believe and know that you can be what you want, do what you want and have what you want.

9. Define your mission. Who are you? What do you love to do? What do you want to be? What do you want to create? How will you serve? How will you create solutions for yourself and others?

10. Itemize what you want. See yourself using all of it. See yourself using all of the good that comes to you – the essence of your rewards and how you will use them for yourself and other people.

11. Empty yourself of mental thinking that keeps you from your dreams, and make room for growth, renewal.

12. Refocus on what is right with your world. Grow, change, learn, expand, experience, every penny you spend should be on growth, health and productivity.

13. Follow your heart, mind and soul, and take steps. Be aware and mindful, and use zeal in your life.

14. Revitalize yourself and be aware and engage life. Try and transform yourself into a rebirth, allow renewal, let go of your old views, study new ideas, expand new perspectives, become reborn in life, be aware of abundance, see abundance, try to see it in everything.

15. Develop a Prosperity Consciousness: See wealth, see prosperity, see beauty of nature, open your eyes to opportunity.

16. If you are going to engage life, you're going to have to think big, use big ideas, and find big solutions.

17. Action: And, once you have these big ideas, and solutions. You need to call people and act on these

solutions, meet with others, communicate, connect to others

18. Deals: Get the deals done that are necessary to put all it altogether, get past your fear, get out of your comfort zone. And if someone says no, kick the dust off your sandals and move onto the next person.

19. Brand: You need to brand yourself and do all you can do to promote your ideas and solutions to the masses, and deliver the best and fastest service. If you can do all these things, you will be great.

Consciousness Exercises

Here are special observations for optimizing your consciousness. Consciousness through certain mental and physical, spiritual practices.

1. There is a collective consciousness and harmonic resonance, and how that affects the individual in their mind and memory. We have a stream of consciousness, and how that thought affects your consciousness in the 21st century, is the C2K. And then there is the spoken word and written word of effect in what you speak and what you write, and how that changes your consciousness going forward after you have made that mental imprint. And then there is controlled visualization, or controlled hypnagogia. Then there is autosuggestion, and how to use repetition in statements of affirmation and decrees to alter and enhance our ongoing mental stream of consciousness.

2. Our essence or being is altered by our thinking and your acting, and habits. Mindfulness, meditation and contemplation affects your consciousness. We can work at emptying or filling our mind with new information.

3. Then there are theories and ideas by greats such as Carl Jung who discussed archetypes and the imprints that are already within you, and what your types of passions, hobbies and work that you tend toward doing based on your archetype or what's in your background. In Vedic Hindu literature, there are many great writings about the energy of: purpose, dharma and even tapas.

4. One key exercise is to improve your consciousness through catharsis, purging, clearing, forgiving, cleansing of your mind and processing information, processing data. Just like a computer processor which has a memory, hard drive and temporary files and cache. We all realize these things need to be optimized to work together.. The same is true with the consciousness, and then there is spiritual energy that animates mind, and how that affects you. How spirituality affects a person.

5. The next exercise would be we have to advance in the type, quality, and nature of our dominant conscious thoughts. We have a choice in the type, quality, and nature of the dominant conscious thoughts that we have, and how do we change our thinking and alter the choices of our thoughts.

6. As an example in Philippians 4 it talks about how to choose what is true and beautiful and right, righteous and so forth. And that is a conscious choice sometimes for many people where we use our power of: will or willingness to direct our thoughts to what is positive.

10 Spiritual and Success Exercises

1. **Visualize Your Day** - At night, review your day – hour by hour. Try to remember what you did from the time you woke up to the end of the day. See each event, each interaction, each relationship. After visualization, consider the things that you could have done better. With this precept of order, much like the spiritual exercises of Ben Franklin over 200 years ago, you may build your character as well as your imagination skills each day.

2. **Contemplative Prayer** - Prayer, breath-work, meditation, visualization, and recognition of health and peace can be taken point by point through the body using a quasi-chakra observance system. When doing the health exercises in this book, you also imagine a healing light going through each chakra region.

Exercise: Sit in a chair or lie down. Close your eyes. Take in air through your nose, hold it for seven seconds, and then let it out of your mouth slowly. Do this at least three times to enter a relaxed state. Clench your fists and extend your fingers as far as they will go a few times and put your hands in your lap. Now clear your mind and imagine a peaceful scene such as a mountain meadow with flowers or a calm lake. Now, begin with the top of your head or crown, or you can also begin with the base or lower body. Go through each of the seven sections in one direction. The first letters of the colors are ROY.G.BIV (red, orange, yellow, green, blue, indigo, violet) with red beginning with the lower body and the head/crown corresponding to the color violet.

Now, go through all seven colors one by one, imaging the color of each chakra and the corresponding section of the body. Imagine each color purifying and regenerating the body, one by one. Relax and purify each section of the body one by one. When you have finished the exercise from crown to lower or lower to higher, release any impure energy to the universe while taking a few breaths from the nose and blowing out from the mouth. Then, express a mental thanks to the Supreme for the healing energy. Then open your eyes.

1. Muladhara (Sanskrit: Mūlādhāra) Lower body - our connection to the earth and the physical plane – Survival and Operation – Color: Red

2. Swadhisthana (Sanskrit: Svādhisthāna) Reproductive gland region of the body – our creative and procreative urges and drives – Color: Orange

3. Manipura (Sanskrit: Manipūra) Stomach/navel - energy center for power and manifestation and desires (location: solar plexus) – Color: Yellow

4. Anahata (Sanskrit: Anāhata) Heart - energy center for love – Color: Green

5. Vishuddha (Sanskrit: Viśuddha) Throat - center for expression – Color: Blue

6. Ajna (Sanskrit: Ājñā) Eyebrow or forehead between brows - our psychic powers – Color: Indigo

7. Sahasrara (Sanskrit: Sahasrāra) Top of head and crown - connection with the Cosmic or the divine. – Color: Violet

8.

3. **Breathing and Purification** – Try to learn the purification breath work. Breathe slowly into your nose and out from your mouth. Imagine negative energy leaving your body with each exhale and see yourself with each intake breath taking in life, love, pure energy, and healing elements.

4. **Sensory Perception** – Learn to feel each part of the body uniquely. Sit or lie down and close your eyes. Then, pick a part of your body. Sense it, feel it, imagine where it is. If a part of your body has aches, pains, or dis-ease, then use this exercise to send healing energy to that spot in a targeted way.

5. **Constructive Journaling** – Every month or every three to six months, sit down and write out things that you are proud of. Write 10 things that you have done to improve your life in recent months. List your best attributes. Write out 5-10 things that you enjoy doing or would like to try. List things that you can do to respect yourself. Even write out a few luxury to-dos where you can take action each year to treat yourself to a trip, family fun, to luxury, or to learning.

6. **COT: Cognitive Occupational Therapy** – Every few days or weeks, you must do things that are cognitive and that involve neuroplasticity exercises. Examples are: learning to recite a poem or prayer, working puzzles, crosswords, or even chores such as unloading the dishwasher, building a model, writing a story, telling a story, preparing and giving a presentation or related activities. The "mind-hand" or "mind-speech" activity is very stimulating and builds mental muscle.

7. **Vibration** - Your vibration can be at many levels. To say the least, you can enhance your mental vibration through various actions. Higher levels of mental and spiritual vibrations include Love, Gratitude, Praise, Faith, Feel Good Emotions, and more. Many practitioners work on a daily basis to enhance and bring their mental and spiritual

vibration to a higher level. Practitioners do this so that they may lead a more harmonious life, but also to attract people, events, and things of the same or higher vibration. The end result of healthy vibrations is the attraction of more constructive events, outcomes, and possibilities.

8. **Euphoric Modeling** – Recall a certain past event or image that brings feelings of joy, happiness, peace, love, or endearment. Have this MOMENT at your beck and call. Whenever you feel a pestering negative thought, seize upon the moment of peace and seek out solutions, forgiveness, and peace of mind.

9. **Cause and Effect** - For every thought, action, or inaction, there is a corresponding thought and event. Your heartfelt emotions when mixed with constructive thought and action carry more force than the average thought and action. Building a foundation is vital to this step. At first, we must change our mentality from one of lack to a consciousness and mind of possibility. Our minds and hearts evolve and begin to believe in opportunity and abundance. Instead of thinking why, we transcend to a spiritual position of why not. At this juncture, we begin to take action in accordance with our dreams. Each mental and physical action we take on a daily basis adds to the momentum of our spiritual force. Our spiritual force in conjunction with our harmonious and constructive thinking begins to manifest higher realities in our days to come.

10. **Habits and Routines** – Develop healthier routines by seeking out activities that build your life and improve your circumstances. Learn to reward yourself for superior habits. Sit down with a trusted advisor and analyze your daily routines. Review your rituals, what you watch, how you exercise, how you think, where you go, who you associate

with, what you do to respect yourself. Evaluate all of these things and then determine how to better treat yourself to a life of excellence, self-regard, transformation, and fewer distractions.

Spiritual Exercises To Expand Creativity, Prescience and Inspiration

1. Basic Prayers for Memory

The first exercise is basic prayers. An example of a basic prayer might be the Serenity Prayer by Reinhold Niebuhr: "God grant me the serenity to accept the things I cannot change, the courage to change the things I can, and the wisdom to know the difference." Many other prayers are perfectly acceptable for all types of spiritual seekers. Many of us use the Sermon on the Mount, which includes the Lord's Prayer or "Our Father".

2. Fellowship Exercise

Seek wise counsel & fellowship. One of the top types of spiritual practice in the 21st century (also in the 20th century) is seeking out other spiritually minded people who want to grow and heal in a spiritual way. There are two parts to this—you are giving of yourself and you are letting others give to you. For instance, you may be going to a spiritual gathering where you could discuss wisdom literature, the Bible, or some other spiritual literature and sharing your experience about it, sharing your interpretation of it, sharing your strength and hope regarding the discussion or mentoring or counseling or coaching or sponsoring other people. The reward to this is you are giving it away, but you are also teaching it. You are teaching about something even as you are learning about something. Therefore, you are giving it away to keep it. If you give of yourself, invariably, you are receiving the rewards of the universe by trying to help other people who are deeply in need.

3. Active Meditation

Active Meditation - Active Meditation involves reading certain meditative literature, absorbing what it means, musing over the literature, thinking about it, and discussing it with other people out loud. Sometimes when you have an active meditation for reading it could be something written like a psalm or a proverb or a Bible passage. You may even have a dictionary available to interpret each word amongst other people, and then you discuss it out loud, but you can read it out loud as well before discussing it. To give you an example, some people may be sitting on a train, maybe reading an article in the newspaper and they put the newspaper down and think about it for several minutes and just allow their body to absorb the information and muse over it and then discuss it later. That's an example of active meditation. And a lot of people think they don't have the ability to meditate, but really most people do because if you just show up somewhere for a spiritual discussion you are in the process of actively meditating over something with other people.

4. Seeking Inspiration and Prescience

This is the practice is praying for inspiration and tapping into your inner divine voice . That is when you can either sit down by yourself and get into a relaxed state and ask the universe for ideas or answers, for God's will, for the ability and the strength to do the right thing, and that's what we mean by praying for inspiration or seeking inspiration. One of the truths about inspiration is, you don't have to act on it; you can seek wise counsel about the inspiration that you've received and ask if it's a good idea. Or, you can just run it through a generalized litmus test. Is the idea or is the inspiration something that will help other people, or something that will be unselfish and loving and good for your heart and your mind? Those are things to ask yourself when you seek inspiration and when you decide to act on the inspiration.

5. Seeking God Consciousness

Praying for the presence of the *Spirit of the Universe* and praying for the presence of God. This includes praying for the energy of God and the spirit of the universe to be with you, to be conscious of it, and to cultivate a God-consciousness. Next, you can seek to develop a harmonious relationship with your universe and with your God and to be at peace with yourself, other people, and with nature. Ultimately, if you can ask for all these things and be open to perceiving them, you will actually find that you have developed a consciousness of love of yourself and the world around you. That is the ultimate goal of most orthodox practitioners of spirituality, and that goal is unity and non-separateness, a unity with your authentic self and unity with God and the world.

6. Mass as a Sacrament

Attending a religious service or mass as a sacramental act. What people overlook is many orthodox spiritual practitioners carry out the ritual of attending a temple or a church or a cathedral or some spiritual house. For the people who attend those services and rituals, those activities are a sacrament, a sacred act. Included in many rituals are singing, chanting, and praying, supplicating, and even circumambulating—a word I like to use that means "walking around." It also refers to the ritual movement of people, whether it be a priest, a rabbi, or other religious leader—the movement of people in a sacred space, asking for and invoking the power and presence of the supernatural into that place of worship—that is a sacrament. The circumambulation, the movement, is certainly a part of the spiritual practice, participating in it, being part of it, and seeing it. Many people actually participate in it by either singing or being part of a choir or being part of the group on the altar that does certain things, and they don't have to be priests, they can just be helping out. So, that is actually a very high orthodox practice.

7. **Absorption Exercise:**

There is a spiritual principle called absorption in Mother Nature, and it happens when plants and animals absorb what is around them. They are able to take in the nutrients, food, and sunlight that they need to grow and to be healthy. As human beings and spiritual beings, one of our primary jobs is to learn to absorb the beneficence of the universe, to absorb what is good around us. That includes the sunlight and the trees and the fresh air and the wonderful scents and aromas that we smell in our environment and the sounds and the noises and the animals and the wildlife and the mountains and the beaches to see it, to feel it, to absorb it, to take it in. This is about learning how to pause and take a deep breath and really draw in life's energy, draw in life's energy. The flip side of that is we need to be able to learn to strategically avoid things that rob us of our energy or steal from us without our permission. I know that's not always possible, but we can strategically avoid toxic situations, toxic people, and toxic encounters and avoid escalating situations where the problem can only get worse. Remember that nine out of ten times great miracles can happen when we just walk away and keep our mouth shut, and there is a time and a place for all of us to stand up for ourselves with or against other situations, issues, or people. But in general, and we need to know, you know, when you are in the presence of another person close your eyes and test how you feel around that other person. Are they taking energy from you? Is there a kindred spirit? Do they help you grow? Do they support you? Do they sustain you? This is not only people, but it can be places and things as well.

With this law of absorption you may need to take a few minutes each morning or each evening before you go to bed, close your eyes and take a few deep breaths and relax each part of the body, and then just consciously think to yourself of what is good in the universe, what good happened to you during the day, what blessings happened. Take some time to think about those people who have been good to you over your lifetime and try and feel that goodwill that came to you, feel that love that someone gave to you in the past. It could be your spouse or your aunt or your uncle, your mother, your father or your brother, your sister, or a teacher. Just think of that one person who gave you love and try to be thankful for that in your heart and in your mind. And remember that each day that supply surrounds us, abundance surrounds us—the air, the water, the life. But we must be open in our heart and in our mind to receiving freely of this supply.

8. **Willingness Exercise:**

The power of willingness. What kind of willingness is good and healthy? What kind of willpower is good and healthy? The short answer is that when you decide and allow yourself to do something and you take that first step of action, you become willing by moving in the direction of your ideas and your dreams. But the really tough part of willingness is that you have to learn to exert your resolve. In doing so, you draw yourself closer to the abundance of the universe and closer to your GOD. , To be willing you have to be able to persist. You have to believe and accept that your goal is possible. Many writers have said the idea wouldn't even be in your mind if it wasn't possible. For many of us it's just difficult to accept and take life's abundance and reach our hands out and let the gift be put in our hands. One famous author used to begin his presentations by holding up $100 bill and saying, "Who wants $100?" It could be a crowd of 1,000 people and finally after 10 or 20 seconds usually one person would finally jump out of their chair and run up there and grab the money. That's the way we have to look at life and sometimes we have to just get up and make our move and take what life is offering us and meet life halfway. Meet Mother Nature halfway. Meet your god and your maker and your creator halfway. Meet the spirit of the universe halfway.

9. Give It Away Exercise:

The power of giving. Giving of yourself builds you up from the inside. Further, we learn things when we teach them. Giving is tangible and intangible and we all benefit if we are able to tithe to others in divinely inspirational ways. We have to be able to give of ourselves the best of ourselves to the universe and the universe will continue to give to us. It doesn't mean you have to donate all your time to charity or donate all of your money to charity, but it does mean that when you are helping others with your spare time or doing the best to support your family and your children, it has a ripple effect on your life and humanity in general. You know, the better you learn to take care of yourself the better you can take care of others. If you learn to take care of your family, you know society will help take care of you.

10. Character Analysis Ritual

Character building is an exercise in itself. The thing we have to remember is that our character is what creates our vibration, and our vibration is what attracts things to our life. We have to continue to build our character and that means adding things to our lives that are good for us on a body, mind, and spirit level. And we have to improve those things, while letting go of the things that hold us back and keep us down. This means letting go of the bad habits that keep us from heading in the direction of our dreams. So, our character attracts the same type of energy to us just like two tuning forks vibrate at the same level. It's a type of resonance. It's how we radiate our good feelings. If we radiate vibrations of excellence and advancement and improvement, people will be attracted to us. When people sense we are giving more to life than we are taking from it, the want to do business with us or even have relationships with us.

Sometimes I counsel people whose lives are in a rut and they are trying to make some big changes are stuck, and I always tell them to be careful about getting into a relationship at this time. You have a better chance of making life changes if you are not trying to develop a new relationship, and likewise, you will be available for a meaningful relationship once you get your inner house in order. A person who is going to the gym, taking care of their body and going to school, taking care of their mind, or taking on a new job and getting new skills, will become more attractive to other people.

The next thought is just about your purpose. All of us have to find meaning in life, and we have to pick a purpose. We have to dedicate ourselves to something and choose the direction we want to go in. This could be choosing big goals or a five- or ten-year goal, or it could just be a one-day goal. In any event, you have to pick something. You have to commit to different activities. We have to commit to different tasks and goals and we have to find our purpose. Purpose for us is what you above all want to accomplish, either today or for the rest of your life. Maybe you can't figure that out right now, but at least write it down this question: "What do I really, really want to do, dedicate myself to?" Maybe it could be some niche idea or topic of study or research, just what do I want to specialize in, or what do I want to be the best at? Once you find that goal and you are ready to go forward and never look back—that's usually what defines greatness. People who can pick something and stay focused on it can become great in that particular area if they are willing to commit to it and dedicate their lives to it and never look back.

11. Awareness Exercise:

Fo anyone to be aware, they need to wake up. Wakefulness means that we need to wake up in our deeper minds and perception abilities. We need to see truth regardless of appearances and we need to lose our sense of separateness from the world and allow ourselves to be part of it and to see it, to feel it, to interact with it and be more and more aware of our surroundings. When we do this, we can become saturated with the idea that there is abundance and prosperity in this world.

12. Association Exercise:

Your Vibration. The law of vibration by association is the principle that says that we become more like the energies that we associate with. The more time you spend with somebody or the more you are in a certain type of environment, the more one you are going to become one with it and the more you are going to identify with a certain group of people, a certain place, or certain types of things.

13. Creativity:

All of us are born with a certain creativity, a certain type of expression. We have to learn to express ourselves and express that God-given talent and learn to express it at the highest level we can. It could be little ideas, it could be little bits of creativity, it could be making little pieces of art, writing little poems, creating special clothing, or making little arts and crafts that people want. Every one of us have our own desires to express ourselves and be our authentic selves and express our authentic purpose. What I'm trying to say to you is that unless we head in the direction of our creativity and use our hands and our minds and our bodies we may become frustrated in life that we are not participating in our ideas and our creativeness that belongs to us. To stimulate creativity, each of us should take time each week to quiet our minds and listen for ideas. Being receptive to guidance. In this way, we can find our purpose and discover our labors of love which will allow us to better serve our families and humanity.

14. Spiritual Gymnasium

Mental and spiritual strength are vital to maintain, and I do believe many of us need to continue in the spiritual gymnasium everyday to continue in that prosperity and abundance workout every day. If you can cultivate a prosperity consciousness that becomes so strong that you are easily able to harvest abundance, then you will have developed real spiritual strength. You have to learn to be so strong as to deny and refute the endless possibilities of something not going your way because it's very easy for us to sit around and say, oh, this is going to happen, this bad is going to happen, or this is not going to go my way. It's so easy to be a nega-holic. But by the same token, if you can focus your mind at looking at all of the possibilities of greatness and wealth and abundance and creativity, then you will be immune from the sickness of negativity.

15. Sacred Days

We should observe sacred days, which could include various holidays: Christmas or Easter, St. Joseph's Day, All Saints/Red Mass, 12th Night, or even May Day. Many of these sacred days are based on the lives of Saints, the lives of the masters or, of course, seasonal festivities. Participation in these festivities may call for different rituals, different types of altars, different types of songs, different types of vestments and attire. Some even have a Festival of Saints, for instance, Semana Santa. People in Spain dress up in special outfits and carry large candles and they have different marching groups, and they go through the town. In some of these cities and towns, whether it be Germany or Austria or Spain, have these sacred festivals. Some of them are hundreds of years old. They're even in different parts of Germany. They have carnival days which some people call Drei Tolle Tage or Three Crazy Days that goes back almost 800 years as it relates to Carnival Karnival. These are sacred days. These festivities allow people to fellowship and congregate and celebrate certain times of the year. Some people even were able to unwind and relax as a by-product of these festivities. And other types of festivities allow them to enter sacred meditation, sacred prayer, sacred communion with either a spiritual master or holy person like the Mother Mary.

16. **Services and Sacred Space**

Another type of ritual is praying the stations of the cross, fasting, or even communion itself. In any of these cases, you may be invoking the Spirit of the Universe, God, or Christ, Mother Mary, or some other master and invoking the presence of that master into your life. And you may also engage in certain types of fasting or dietary restrictions as a symbol of sincerity. With communion and during masses and liturgies, the priests are invoking the presence and the actual energy of God into the alter and congregation, and they're administering that sacred energy or communion to individuals to help unite them with the Holy Spirit as well as remove their sins and help protect them from wickedness.

17. **Nature Bound and Pilgrimages and Commitments**

We can all benefit from the practice of retreat or a time-out or a visit with nature, or even a committed rehabilitation of some sort. There are people who actually take vows with a certain organization perhaps as a monk or an oblate. These are different types of specialized higher rituals with higher degrees of commitment. I've know many families who go on annual retreats together. Some of them are quiet retreats. Some of them are active retreats where they're at a place and eating with others. This type of communal activity is a way to get quiet and relax and get back to the roots of your faith and your life and help draw closer to God and nature. Another example might be a pilgrimage of some sort, such as a hadj or people in Europe that are traveling to a holy place. Some people go to holy places of healing and ask for healing, whether it be in France or Germany or Jerusalem or wherever. In Japan there's these holy places that people go to so they can seek out the energy. Some people refer to these holy places as energy centers. If you've ever been to the top of a pyramid, say in

Central America, and felt the energy of that, you would know exactly what I'm talking about. An example of that would be the pyramid in Tepotzlan, Mexico where you can crawl to the top of the mountain. It's a fantastic little way to commune with nature and the heavens. There's actually steps that go up to the top of that mountain.

18. Communing with Yourself

Now another facet of a retreat would be an individualized type of retreat. If you look at the old Celtic, Viking, and Norse literature, there were people there that would go sitting. They would do what is called sitting out and commune with themselves. They invoke the presence of nature and they would seek out the inspiration and guidance of the Fetch, which would be the animal part of their soul. Some people relate most to a lion or a bear or an eagle. You can go out into nature and commune with whatever animal part of your nature that you feel closest to. It's different than the clan part of your soul that they call the Sippe. The Fetch, the part of your animalistic part of your soul, is what some people also consider your guardian angel. Many people consider that they have a guardian angel. In some other cultures, that guardian is believed to be an actual animal itself or that animal part of your soul, which is fascinating. Some people refer to that in mystical books as the elemental body.

So, these are various types of things you can do to commune with yourself and nature and God: retreats, rehabilitation and sitting out, pilgrimages, and taking in nature, or a nature trip. All of these are ways to get closer to God and to yourself and to Earth.

19. Catharsis and Purification

Around the world, regardless of culture and spirituality or tribe, there are groups that form different purification rituals. These rituals could be done when a baby is born or comes of age to be baptized. Purification could be done through either water or submersion into water, or it could be done through the application of an ointment **** or smoke. If you've ever seen Native Americans, sometimes they can smudge a person or blow smoke on them to purify them and their body or purify a room. That's just an example of clearing. In the Celtic and Viking literature you'll see different types of magical clearing of space where they perform clearing of an area. They could clear to the north and the south and the east and the west. The geographical points, of course, were in the upper and the lower, you'll see that in a Native American seven-direction type exercise. So the purification practices are utilized in various cultures globally.

What I find interesting is that in the Ancient East, including India, purification involves two actions: catharsis: cleansing and emptying. However, in the ancient literature, it also included a practice of FILLING, and I think filling is one of the most overlooked aspects of spiritual catharsis which involves cleansing and purification. Let's say you've been through a tough life and you've had some fears and resentments and some angers and some ideas related to the past that you want to let go; there are two ways to do it. You can try to empty yourself and let go of those issues, those ideas and thoughts, but you can also start filling your mind and your heart with new ideas, new affirmations, new decrees, new empowerments, and new ways of thinking. That also leads to new habits and new actions. Our character is about the totality of our thinking and action and omissions, three different areas; but if you are able to develop new thinking and new habits, you can affect your character. So, developing new ideas, forming new beliefs, and forming new habits, that's really a process of magic that changes us at the core of our being. It changes our DNA structure and it changes our neural pathways, all of that is augmented and changed. And even our future is changed as a by-product of it because if you can continue to clear yourself and add only what's good for you and healthy for you into your life, it affects your life moment to moment and into the future as well. Because if you continue to do good things in the moment then many times it has a ripple effect into the future and with what you think each day in the way you wake up each morning.

20. Contemplative Action

Become contemplative in action. That means to become mindful of the universe while you are engaging in life's activities, not only mindful but connected to the energy of the universe. Connected to the positive source, which most people call God, so you're connected and contemplative while in action. You're mindful while you're working, and you're connected to that perfect energy. One of the keys to being mindful is to be more aware while you are connected.

So, you're trying to do the right thing, while also being more aware of your surroundings at any given moment, more aware of what's going on inside you. More aware of what's going on outside of you. With that higher awareness, with that higher connection, you're operating at a higher level, and you're not missing out on the signs and symbols and miracles of life, and the gifts that come to you and the people that are sent to you. All of that is extremely important when remaining contemplative in action. It's like being in a meditative state while being active at the same time.

21. Daily Meditations and Daily Prayers

Daily spiritual ritual including morning and evening prayers and seasonal prayers. Regardless of what faith and spirituality you are there's probably some good books that can help you in developing your daily meditations, your daily prayers, your daily devotions. All of this is there to help you get into the alpha state, get into the meditative state each day, and become connected to your world and become at peace with yourself and other people. Take a few deep breaths and really prepare for your day, and take time in the evening to prepare to go to sleep, and see if you can be a better person in the next day.

Now, a daily ceremony can also mean just a book that you read and meditate over when you're doing your daily prayers. Many people also attend a daily service or an evening or morning mass they could go to with a few people, and that way they're able to pray and commune with each other. They have a little service where they're able to ask for help, and ask for forgiveness, and for empowerment to be of service to the world and to their family.

22. Meditative Objects

There are many ways to use icons, prayers cards and meditative objects and services. This is very interesting. I don't know if you've ever walked in on a maze, a spiritual maze, and taken the steps according to the actual little walk and made the prayers in each little section of the maze, but that's just an example of a prayer type of activity related to yourself, and to the given place. The other thing is with icons, you may have little icons on your desk or in your home that remind you of a spiritual master or a god or a holy mother or Buddha or whatever it might be. The point of that is just to recognize and be able to have that consciousness or higher power.

Prayer cards are something smaller. Of course, you can keep them in your wallet or in your purse and they may have a beautiful picture on one side and a prayer on the other side. And it's something you can hold and physically look at and pray. If there's a special prayer on one side for protection or whatever, it could be a saint on the card, or it could be Jesus Christ, it could be Lakshmi, the goddess of progeny and abundance from India, it doesn't matter. The point being is that it's a physical object that allows you to stay connected. You're not worshipping the object. You're just using it as a reminder and a mental refresher of your commitment to being spiritually connected. In addition, there are services that are less liturgy oriented, and they're more meditative oriented. If you've ever been to a Taize service, you'll understand that it's a type of meditative service in a regular Christian Church where you try and meditate on an object and an idea in quietude.

23. Spiritual Jewelry and Charms

Another type of personal ritual and practice that many people have is just the collection of spiritual charms to wear whether it be a necklace or a bracelet, or something to hold in your pocket or a keychain, or it could be anything like that or some type of medallion. I'm sure some people may even use an earring or some other type of ring, but that's beside the point. I'm not really talking so much about charms and amulets. I'm mainly talking about reminders, reminders of protection and the power of protection, and the power of blessings that you may want to carry with you or wear on your body.

An example would be the cross of St. Benedict. It's a fantastic cross, and it has the Latin words inscribed up and down the cross that a lot of people don't know, but it says "The cross will protect me that goes before me" on one side of it, and on the other side of the cross it says that "No demon will be able to get me." So, it's kind of a fantastic little charm that goes back probably 300 or more years which is really amazing in one particular faith. And that's just one example of a type of charm or a cross that is carried by certain people.

24. Energy Centers

There are an abundance of holy and sacred places, for example: a Chapel, a Hindu Temple, Pyramid, Cathedral, or a other sacred edifice. For instance, I remember once going to a large place of worship, a citadel in Cairo, and going in there to pray, and it's just a fantastic experience and I did the same in Singapore with a Hindu temple. It doesn't matter where you are around the world. In Latin America, I remember going to say some prayers on the top of a Mayan Pyramid or an Aztec Temple. I later found that this Pyramid was known for its local warrior god of which many people still pray toward today. So, these are just examples of sacred places that many people today call "energy centers" around the world that people like to visit as a sacred pilgrimage of sorts.

25. Higher Self Visitation Exercises

There are vast exercises used to cultivate a relationship with your higher self, and one of the exercises and rituals that I've seen is to commune with yourself in a visual way. You would do a visualization or an enhanced meditation where you see yourself meeting with your higher self in a sacred place to commune.

Communing with yourself is an "inner transformation" or doppelganger type of exercise, because you're meeting with your higher self or your double. To begin this "meet your authentic self" exercise requires your relaxed imagination. Some people may see themselves as a bird or a falcon flying through the sky, through the forest and landing at the sacred place. Then they morph back into their bodies or into a human being who then walks to the sacred door. Upon opening the door they walk into a great hall and see this other self of theirs up on a throne or maybe at the end of a table, and they sit down and talk to that other self. That other self can look like yourself or it can look like another race; it can have long dark hair, long blonde hair, it can have a crown, or it can be a man or a woman, it doesn't matter. It's what you feel your higher self or higher source would look like. It's part of your soul.

You ask that person questions, deep questions, questions you want to answer, maybe advice, and it may give you something deeper and more authentic than even your own wisdom. It may be able to give you calmer and more sincere answers to questions that you are seeking to answer. The answers may even be different or modified in some way than the ones that you've already come up with by yourself. So, it's a fantastic exercise. Or you could just go there to be thankful, and to be safe with this person, and to commune with this other side of yourself, this higher side that is tapped into the source of all energy.

26. Mantras

Short or memorized prayers can be as simple as a prayer that you've either written by yourself or someone else has written, like the serenity prayer by Reinhold Niebuhr, which is quite famous, or the St. Joseph prayer or any other great prayer. People may use it as a mantra, or just a short prayer that you just may use one word, like God or prosperity or whatever, and you can say this again and again to yourself, silently in meditation or during the course of your day and that's an example of a prayer mantra that you may have.

27. Prayer for Others and Forgiveness

Praying for others is extremely important, and that includes internal and external forgiveness. Many people pray for the welfare of their loved ones or family, their children, their relatives, and so forth, and then there's other types of prayers. You may want to pray for somebody who is a leader or pray for someone you dislike or pray for someone that you want to forgive, whether they're living or not living. People who have gone into group therapy or private therapy may at times send a letter to someone or leave a letter on someone's tomb or even facilitate a rite of penitence.

28. Hospitality Exercise

Another type of spiritual practice or ritual would be just hospitality and this goes back really to the ancient peoples of many cultures, whether it's an Eskimo culture or a German culture or a Russian culture. I'm just giving you some examples. When a stranger comes to your door and they're hungry, that type of hospitality, feeding the individual, the traveler, with food and drink and hospitality and maybe even a place to sleep, all of these things are important. I think maybe today hospitality has been transformed into helping making sure people have a safe place to stay and some healthy food to eat when they're in need. It's very, very important. In its highest form, hospitality honors those who are contributing to humanity and you give or tithe to others to support their good works.

29. Celtic Action

Many Celtic prayers are based in action and activities. There are examples of people who say little prayers along with their actions. They may say a prayer when they do the harvest or a prayer when they serve dinner or a prayer when they kill a beast that will be used to feed the family or the tribe. I'm giving you some shamanic examples, but these are just examples of how specialized prayers are used for everyday activities and everyday events.

30. Sabbath

Having a sacred day during the week is generally know as Sabbath. It could be on Sunday, but in other cultures it may be Friday or a Saturday or another day. Whenever it is, it's having quality time to either take care of yourself or take care of your family members or your children or to commune with nature or to be silent or even in some cultures to commune with your ancestors or those that have gone before you. These are all examples of how the Sabbath is important. Many people attend mass or a church service or a temple or other type of service. So all of this is part of keeping one day special where you can rest and recuperate and be prepared for the rest of your week.

31. **Environmental Exercise**

The section is about an eco-ritual or environmental harmony that's based on many Shamanic cultures, but particularly some of the pagan cultures of ancient Europe and Asia and in Africa. It involves having environment respect and respect for animals, much like the Native Americans did, and respecting the trees and the plants and the crops and even like I had read a book by Thich Nhat Hanh once and he even talked about it. He's a famous Buddhist Monk and he even talked about how he ate his meals he would sometimes pray while eating or pray before or after eating, pray in thankfulness to all the animals and the trees that worked in harmony to create his food. So, all of us want to keep nature unpolluted and protect our forests and our rivers and our mountains, and environmental respect goes back and is a timeless part of spirituality and respect from the beginnings of time until now in many cultures. Trees and other things have been used, either before Christ or afterwards, in the use of sacraments or rituals.

32. **Character Exercise**

The section is about precepts or character building and this is about a ritual. Whether you look at Marcus Aurelius or Ben Franklin, or at the present moment people like Steven Covey, you're looking at your daily activities and how you can be a better person each day and maybe you might make a list at the end of the day of the things you did well and the things you didn't do well and see if you can improve on them. In 12-step lingo, the 10th step focuses on being a good person each day and trying to be good to others and make amends to others when you can. Even if you read the writings of Pythagoras or Buddha you would see this same type of character building virtues in their practices, and with Socrates as well, in virtues and ethics in their daily lives.

33. Tithe Exercise

Giving and receiving is part of our world. Generosity and giving are timeless activities based on love and compassion. There are 2 types of giving. 1) giving to those who need help 2) giving to those who are expanding their talents, abilities, and craft. Either type of giving is inherently good. Practice giving your time or money to that which inspires you divinely.

The Process of Magic and Manifesting

1. As beings that desire increasing life, we each contain energies of body, mind and spirit of which we must maintain equilibrium between all three energies. To preserve this balance we utilize our threefold powers. Use of mental, spiritual and physical powers in a spiritual way must produce abundance.
2. All thoughts begin with an idea which is the byproduct of divine connection to the source of all thought.
3. The ideas in back of the thought are the mystical form of all creation and the underpinnings of tangible results or manifestation.
4. When you harmonize your mental state, your individual connection to the universe of ideas is expanded.
5. All thoughts tend to lead to the field of potential outcomes for all actions, inactions, and creation.
6. Deep Thinking or what is believed in mind habitually becomes who you are and is your essence or character.
7. Free will creates Choices where commitments must be selected. We all have the ability to choose how we use free will in terms of thoughts and actions.
8. Choices create the nucleus of new form and begin a chain reaction if the choice is fueled with emotion and belief.
9. Emotions that fuel manifestation are love, joy, peace, happiness, goodness, and other positive emotions.
10. When each idea is transformed into a intention, then each intention may be transformed into a plan, vision, and mission. Then it is chosen as a prime objective for the individual
11. When the plan is primus it becomes a purpose which is backed by belief.
12. When firm belief, earnestness and constructive emotion are in back of a purpose, it is energized.
13. Our belief system must be based on the constant and creative possibility of optimal results and prosperity. Everyone who is living upright in a spiritual way is deserving and capable of tapping into this abundance.

14. We become best at co-creating our destiny when we are in spiritual unity with the universe where a person develops the realization of the Divine Presence within one's own self.
15. We operate most effectively when we are awakened and clear in mind. Attunement and forgiveness of ourselves and others allows us to be free of anger and to live in the present moment fully in an awakened state of mind.
16. Acceptance - We must believe that prosperity and well-being is our birthright.
17. Believe that you have wealth and freedom and that you are the essence of creative ability.
18. Everything that is needed is continually provided by an ever expanding world and universe that is abundant and impersonal.
19. We must understand the essence or rationale behind the purpose of each desire that we want to cultivate.
20. Further, we must comprehend in some way how our big ideas will help others along with ourselves to convey the sincere impression of value, worth, and increase.
21. Before implementing each plan or taking any big step, we evaluate our mental effectiveness. Getting clear and going thought a catharsis of mind. This means to look at your track record, atone, prune, purge, and clear away the mental debris. Begin to use "what works" and start to utilize the best practices which make you efficient.
22. Clear Objectives - Set specific goals, research and refine them. After the purpose, task and objective is clear, then push forward with persistence.
23. Results Driven. What is the mission, destination, vision. Develop affirmations that correlate to the most favorable end-result.
24. Think, feel and act "AS IF" you are already in possession of the life that you want. Cultivate your emotions and your

character around the "As If". You must become what you want which means you become the person who owns the life you desire.
25. Look at where you are, where you are going and periodically reset the course and navigation to optimize the journey.
26. Learn to think and speak in a prosperous way that conveys peace, abundance, and increase. Mold the habits and tendencies of your thought. Refuse to accept lack and fear.
27. Take action. Keep lists and do three things toward your dreams per day, do them constructively to the best of your ability.
28. Study your life, reflect on your day, decide how to continually improve yourself. Do your homework and do all you can to learn and know your purpose, objectives and master your skills. Be the best at what you do and BE Known for your excellence.
29. Meditations and Prayer - Write out affirmative meditations such as, "Each day I am improving". Write out 10 statements that are affirming and positive. Contemplate over them each day. You can write out generalized affirmations or very specific ones.
30. Use the affirmative statements or contemplation, to increase acceptance of our potential and boost our awareness.
31. Visualize - See yourself in optimal circumstances in your mind's eye and Feel it. If you can visualize the optimal result, then see the next step. Example. See yourself a few pounds leaner toward your optimal weight.
32. Choose your environment. Select what to feed yourself. Mold your circumstances by your actions and specific thought.
33. Organize your affairs. Gain the habit of finishing things well. Become excellence, simplify your life, empty the clutter, and redefine your focus. Develop prosperity based routines.

34. Imprint and affirm your ideals and dreams into your consciousness. The plan, desired thing, or result must be written and then verbalized. It should be claimed into this world using the spoken word.
35. Make wealth and excellence a priority. Align your thoughts to attract excellence and wealth. Be aware, be open, learn to receive from others, offer praise, and appreciate life. Accept your potentiality, gifts, and abundance.
36. Circulate your GOOD. Service and Giving - Donate time or money to people or organizations who are the source of your spiritual sustenance.
37. Sixth Sense - Learn and practice creativity, awareness, and contemplation. Keep a journal, write out ideas, develop and allow a universal flow of inspiration and ideas into your life.
38. Review and remember your actions. Reflect on what you have done well each day and things you may not have excelled upon. Be determined to be better and do the right thing. Over 200 years ago, Ben Franklin worked his precepts of order each evening. He wanted to be excellent and build his character even at a mature age.
39. Research ideas - What are your passions, how do your ideas serve? Listen to your intuition & cultivate strategy. Look at what it would take to implement or be successful with your new ideas: then act on them, implement the plan, review the plan and then improve it.
40. List out streams of income and potential ways to serve and be prosperous. List how you will expand your life. Go past your comfort zones. List goals beyond your expectations and have deadlines of specificity. You can always change the date.
41. Review your lists and projects. Check off your accomplishments.
42. Meet with partners, family and/or spouse to define goals.

43. Discover your natural expression. What is your labor of love. Where do your passions lie. Remember that you work to pay bills, but you should always follow your dreams. Devote 20 percent of your waking hours each week to your passion. If you become great at it, odds are you can earn a living doing it too.
44. Character - How do you want to BE.? Self respect and self regard can be developed and nurtured. When you rebuild yourself, you will in-turn love yourself better which allows you to be kinder, more generous, and more loving to others.
45. With Character comes responsibility toward your mental, physical and spiritual health. Do what works to take care of yourself with: diet, exercise, learning, sleep, study, and fellowship.
46. Associate with those who can help you where you can also help them. Create a network of business and spiritual friends.
47. Be good to your self. Learn health self regard and cultivate a loving relationship with the Source.
48. Teaching others - Giving it away to keep it.
49. Law of Increase and Charisma - Radiate abundance, cheer and enthusiasm. Be contagious with love, cheer, and enthusiasm.

The Power of Consciousness in the Now - Presumption Decoded

Being Contemplative in Action – Getting Into NOW

If you have ever thought deeply about the magical power of the present moment, you may wonder if you have the capability of this type of superior focus and mindfulness. After reviewing all of the major religions on the philosophy on the power of PRESENCE, I have discovered many specific keys to success in being in the moment. To begin with, the theme of the Power of Awareness is to quiet the mind, to calm the self-talk, to learn to control your thoughts while directing your thinking so that you may be present in the moment, to be alive and conscious "right now".

This is not necessarily a Eastern or Western concept, however there are many esoteric & Christian underpinnings herein that are addressed. Firstly, it is advised that we intently listen to our self-talk deep within our mind and then try to truly see and listen to that inner-voice as an observer. Getting to know your ego voice as compared to your authentic spiritual voice of your heart is also a major exercise of this topic.

The easiest example of directing your awareness to the now is to direct your controlled attentiveness to your body, to your breathing, to what you see, what you hear, what you're eating or what you're tasting or who you're with. Whether it's focusing on the aliveness of your child or actually seeing or sensing parts of your own body, you can go deeper into your awareness.   Here's an example: Try to actually feel your extremities, actually noticing the feelings in your fingers or feelings in your toes at any given moment. Or, what emotions are going on in your mind or even in your stomach.

If you're like the average person, your mind could be harping on 50 different things at once, like a TV on 50 different channels constantly running, and the real key is to pick a channel and focus on a single concept, one thing at a time, one moment at a time, one day at a time, one instance at a time. Further, we can concentrate on one thing at a time, or we can just be aware to the moment and allow our mind to do what is best for us.   As an example, the famous movie The Last Samurai with Tom Cruise, they were talking about no mind. To NOT overthink everything is what a teacher would mean by no mind, not overthinking every single move or every single tactic. And just like driving, the first time you drive the car or stick shift, there's many things that you're learning how to do that sooner or later becomes something embedded in your subconscious or in your machinery, and you automatically can get in a car and know exactly what you need to do. So the key really is to be able to program the way you live to think and live in a way that doesn't require you to overthink everything. This process allows you to exist in your real-time state of aliveness.

After rereading books on mysticism and self empowerment, many of us have an awakening of consciousness, a spiritual awakening of sorts, and don't even know how it happened or what had happened and years later we figure out that as a byproduct of reading what other mystics had taught about these types of transformations, we become better people. However, there are many of us out here in the world who have already had this similar type of awakening, this aliveness, this consciousness, and if you are one of us, you know it deeply. If you're on an enlightened path, you will inherently know it because you can walk in a room with 100 people in it, and you can look around and you actually see people and you're actually alive and you actually know what is happening. And if you're living in this awake-ness, you will have the ability to control what's going on in your mind and your thoughts, and you will have the ability to choose and decide the type of thinking that you will have all day long, and in the end the type of thinking that you have all day long, the type of actions you do all day long, the person who you are, who you become all day long. Then that's who and what you REALLY are. That is what you will become. So in total, if you're able to control your thinking and you're able to control who you are and the totality of your actions and inactions; then, you're entirely able to control your destiny and you're able to control what you become.

In books such as the Power of Now, Teachers such as Eckhart Tolle spend a lot of time talking about "no mind" and pain body. And I'm just going to explain it to you right now. Pain body is basically Eckhart Tolle's way of saying that if you're one of these people that's sitting around each day thinking negative thoughts and destructive thoughts and trying to be the victim and trying to identify with all this negative stuff and complaining all the time while also trying to blame everyone except yourself or your situation, That is the pain body. You can learn about ego related negativism in church, from a life coach, or in various spiritual venues. However, Tolle's book s was the most popular manuscript to codify the concepts.

And what I'm saying is that if you have this ego that's wrapped up in this identity and it's trying to protect itself, it's not going to want to take a look in the mirror. Your ego is not going to want to change. It's not going to want to accept responsibility for your life and the way you are and what's become of you. So if you can break free of that ego bondage and find your spiritual self, your true inner self, who you really are and get in touch with that and get in touch with the spirituality within, then all the sudden this unlimited flow and this unlimited potentiality becomes available to you, and that's where this aliveness comes from. And, that's what the Christians talk about being *contemplative in action* and also Christians also talk about the Holy Spirit, which is basically that connectedness and that non-separateness, that *spiritual, god-unity* that every religion around the world talks about.

Once you enter this aliveness and this newfound awakening and this consciousness, you'll have no need to defend yourself. You'll have no desire to overreact to things. You'll have this true power within. And also you'll have this now consciousness, which determines how you effectively manifest things. Let's put it this way: if you're able to develop a new consciousness of aliveness, a higher consciousness of success, a greater consciousness of action and doing things, this **_"in the moment"_** consciousness is what will transmute ideas into success and transform possibility into taking mental form, bring ideas into material tangible form on this plane.

In many other religions or spiritual movements, you'll hear the word 'acceptance' and being able to accept what is. It is what it is or accept the now or accept the good and accept the bad and let go of it. Because this is in essence what will free you from present pain in the mind that's saying that you should be in pain.

Furthermore, this idea of knowingness is what you really want. You want to know and believe that you could control your destiny, and if you don't know and you don't believe, then you might be sitting around wishing for something to happen or hoping for something to happen, and it can keep you stuck in the past, or the future. And it can keep you from realizing your dreams if your ego and your "self" is so identified with things that are wrong with the world. If you can change your train of thoughts and change how you think, you'll be able to have your mind focus on what is right with the world and look at what is good and what is beautiful. And if you start focusing on all the good and the beautiful and the rightness and the righteousness of the world and its impersonal nature, you'll be able to attract more of that.

The Power of Esoteric Spirituality and Metaphysics

In essence, developing metaphysical power is an inside job. This is an esoteric science, this power of now. So being able to control what goes on the inside is esoteric and it's what spiritual and religious and philosophical leaders have been talking about since Pythagoras, Socrates, Plato, Confucius, Buddha, Aristotle and all the rest. They've been talking about these metaphysical concepts since the beginning of civilization. If you can master yourself, you'll be able to master your destiny and have a great effect upon those around you and do a great service for humanity.

What is great about The Power of Now or being in the moment with your consciousness, it allows you to compartmentalize the day, which keeps you from being paralyzed by any situations and you're able to free the mind of attachments. And if you can free the mind of too much junk that's floating around in it, you're able to focus and concentrate and direct your energies into the areas that will most improve your life from the inside out.

Additionally, attention is energy, so you need to remember what you focus on expands in your life. You need to choose and decide what to energize with your attention in any given moment. So like I said before, the pain body is this negative energy of the ego mind, and if you're able to get your attention away from that and give your attention to things that are constructive and positive and reinvigorating, then that's what you want to do because if you give your attention to the pain body, guess what? That's fuel that will keep pain flowing and going. Those who teach about the power of the PRESENT also write a lot about how your conscious mind and your subconscious mind coexist, or rather, how to transcend your ego elf to begin to listen to your spiritual voice.

It's like this, all of us really need to tap into that spiritual self, which is basically the best friend that you had growing-up when you were child. Now you know that there's an old adage that says that some children have their little best friend, their *imaginary* friend, which is really their spiritual higher-self that they are embracing and befriending and their imagination allows them to love that part of themselves without limitation. However, a lot of children lose that magical relationship at a very early age.

We know this story. We've seen it time and time again, so we know that this spiritual self, this best friend, that's the relationship that we need to cultivate. The relationship with our spiritual self and our relationship with the spirit of the universe should come first for us to maximize our peace and prosperity.

So anyway, some of these famous authors of days gone by have said that when you have a grateful mind and a thankful heart, it is a lot easier to have a living faith. Thus a mind of joy cannot support pain body or negative thinking. So the best thing that we can all do for ourselves to change our worldview is to change how we think and change our state of gratitude. As the famous philosopher Magus Incognito once said, each person's worldview is based on their spiritual condition.

So the word 'alchemy' really is transmuting one substance into another substance, and here if you could change your lower self into your higher self, if you could transcend from your ego into your spiritual essence, that is the real key to these teachings. Transmutation is achieved by the conscious contact with the spirit of the universe. Transmutation is achieved through the consciousness of love, the consciousness of wisdom, the consciousness of gratitude and joy.

The other issue in the power of the moment is how many of us are addicted to the adrenaline of anger or self-righteousness or justified anger and blame, and unfortunately that's why social justice has become such a trendy thing is because it can get you so riled up about blaming somebody for something that happened a long time ago when in essence if we focused all that very same time and energy for inner social justice, the whole world would probably change for the better.

And the other thing of this is that if we surround ourselves with sick people, angry people, people who are not alive, people who are realists, who think the world is bad, that type of attitude is contagious, and unfortunately as spiritual seekers, we want to be close to those who want a spiritual life.

And if we can draw close to those who have the same general desire of wholeness and aliveness and health, then we will all become healthier much quicker, and this of course is why self-help groups and fellowships of sorts have become so popular over the last 30, 40, 50 years.

And really the theme of NOW reminds of flow, reminds me of detachment. Meister Eckhart talked a lot about detachment. And we're talking about non-resistance, and there's just so many times in our lives where you can just let go and thrive. Accordingly, some of the biggest miracles in our lives happen when we're not fighting something, we have our mouths shut and we just allow things to pass us by. We have to know when to FLOW and when to pick our battles and know when to stand up for ourselves, but in general, 99% of the time we're going to be okay if we can just stay calm in the moment and allow people to just be.

Once you have developed this aliveness and this consciousness, this higher order in your life, you know what it tastes like and you're going to want more of it, and you're going to do the things that you can do to stay in tune and embrace and own it because it feels so good to be alive and to be clear and if we keep our minds somewhat clear and we do the things we need to do each day or each week to maintain like to spirit, that clarity and that peace of mind will be available and afforded to us.

In the end, this is about surrender. It's about "surrender to win". If you let go of the things that are hurting you, you're able to move forward and not have to drag a lot of dead weight along with you anymore. And then you'll learn to act with purpose and clarity and focus because you're not carrying all this useless baggage. And, then you'll learn to do all you can in the now. And this surrender really unveils your spiritual power.

So in essence, a lot of religions and movements, spiritual groups talk about this key to power, being free and clearing the mind. When you're able to master yourself, you're able to let go of all the junk in the past, you're able to create this space inside of you and allow some joy and greatness to come into your life for the first time. Some people refer to it as a spiritual vacuum, and this vacuum, once you clear stuff out, it creates space in a vacuum and something has to fill it. And if you're in the power of now and you have this consciousness of good and you believe and you know that the world will take care of you in spite of everything that's going on, then good things will come to you. Good people, good ideas, good opportunities, good health and so forth will all be available to you.

So in summary, what is The Power of Now to me and what can it be to you? It's developing this relaxed and free awareness of the now, of the moment and in that relaxed free awareness you become receptive and awake to the good and the beautiful things in the world such as gratitude, health, aliveness, optimism, knowingness, and you're "I am-ness" or "spiritual and divine energy/presence" is made available to you. And what is the "I am"? The "I am" is your presence, is your spiritual self that is talked about in the old wisdom literature. And you become conscious of the now field of energy, which you will master and learn to control what is in that energy, that totality of it, and that becomes who you are.

And if you're anything like me or other people, when you wake up one morning, after having been engaging gratitude in your daily life and you begun clearing the baggage out of your past and using these methods and these steps of developing clarity, you begin letting go of all of the mental rubbish or clutter that has weighed you down. Then, you will find that you want to practice gratitude on a daily basis, you start to practice peace of mind on a daily basis and cultivating a thankful heart and a thankful mind on a daily basis. And behold, one morning sometime soon you're going to REALLY wake up and you're going to wake up on the RIGHT side of the bed, and you're going to KNOW it. And then a few days later, if you keep practicing this consciousness of love and consciousness of God and consciousness of good, you might wake up again like that, and then all of the sudden you'll continue to wake up on the right side of the bed and you'll look forward to the days and you'll be alive and want to do things each day for yourself and other people and participate in life.

And all of that aliveness and that now-ness and that spiritual awakeness is what dissipates this pain body and this negative thinking.

So in conclusion, you and a lot of other people, once you become awake, you're going to be so thrilled and energized by it that you're going to be changed, you're going to want to repudiate generalized negative thinking, and if you hear other people talking about negative thinking and pessimistic stuff and wasteful stuff, you're not going to want to be around them. What I'm saying, if you hear your own voice in your mind and you're observing your mind complaining and trying to justify and blame and seek all this stuff, you're going to tell it to stop. You're going to want to wake up alive and on the right side of the bed and in tune with the infinite and connected to the world, and you're going to want to wake up and see the beauty of life, and regardless of what bad things happen.

And if you're anything like me or most people in general, we have all had some big challenges..... I've gone through tragedies like Hurricane Katrina. I've lost loved ones, including my father. I've lost businesses, had people steal lots from me, and I've had burdens just like everyone else. I've had losses and defeats and pain and real catastrophic events in my life, but when you achieve this aliveness and this consciousness of now, you know that you can move on and you can prevail and even go to greater heights regardless of what happens because you truly have yourself and you have your unity, your empowerment, and your earnest connection to the Spirit of the Universe.

Power of Past and Present

Historically, there are nuggets of truth that many do not know about the power of now. And, through my studies of ancient shamanism in different parts of Asia and Northern Europe, the ancient peoples really did believe that the now is manifested here both in logic and language. And, these Northern tribes believed in only a past and a non-past, and there's no future until you have acted. So, in essence what that means is that "the now creates the future", or the now is the future as a byproduct of the past and present action. So thus, every moment of thought and action becomes the future, the present, and the past which guides and determines a set of pre-destinies or outcomes with variables that may be enhanced by the mind, body, and spirit.

Spiritual Filling and Re-Charging

There is a field of potentiality in the spiritual vacuum, but mind must be organized and cleansed to have that force and pressure to be effectively applied. Thus, when we want to create a new opportunity or new destiny, we need to realize that we need to purge ourselves in one of 2ways: either that or forcefully fill ourselves with some new information or new good or new ideas to push out the old, or we need to empty and clear our mind and heart and then allow new ideas and good to enter. And, must realize that IN nothing IS something. What that means is nothing is a blank page of your day or your life, and in that vacuum of nothingness it acts like a magnet that is supercharged by intent. So, a blank piece of paper, for instance, in your mind, the picture screen of your mind can be charged with your intent. And, that can become something in the supernatural world of your mind. Furthermore, it is your consciousness or your I-am-ness, or your "is-ness" that creates your consciousness. But, it's also the co-creator and manifestor of your experience and your journey. So basically, your consciousness, or your is-ness, or your mindfulness creates and manifests your experience. So, your worldview or your mental view of the world creates your journey.

Clear Your Mind – Banishing Negativity for Abundance

The Steps of Attunement. The clearing away of mental debris through a process of self-analysis and attunement will allow us to obtain greater peace of mind and mental effectiveness toward abundance.

1. **Remain Teachable:** Keep right-sized with regard to our ego.
2. **Developing Character:** Seek change and be open to growth. Eliminate what is not useful and adapt for new abilities
3. **Honesty and Integrity:** Do what you say and be honest with yourself.
4. **Purity of Thought:** Keep your thinking clear, act in the now, and enjoy each moment.
5. **Be Selfless:** Give without expectation of return through service and non-hoarding of things and yourself. Circulate your goodness and radiate your excellence.
6. **Develop Higher Purpose:** Making healthy decisions to have a definite purpose toward your objectives or advancement for all.
7. **Appreciation:** Be thankful for the gifts you have received, praising others and blessing your home, family, and world.
8. **Reflection:** Maintain a willingness to engage self-analysis and evaluation for the purposes of growth.
9. **Attunement:** Seek harmony to heal disputes with others through amends, restitution, mental catharsis, character development, and right action.
10. **Visualization:** Use contemplation, prayer, or meditation to enable a mental vision of a fuller life and connection to the universe. Apply constructive meaning to present or past events.
11. **Open Mind:** Keep the motivation to be open-minded about accepting a state of well-being and peace.
12. **Love and Harmony:** Allow peace and tranquility in your life, and embrace a sincere belief that life is abundant and that love and harmony can be allowed into your heart permanently

Prayers for Protection, Love, Forgiveness and Health

Protection Prayer – Recite 3X
Father's Love, Forever Bright
Divine Mothers' Emerging Light
Surround My Soul With your Affection
Your Super Power Gives Me/Us Protection

Love Prayer – Recite 3X
Mighty Peace is in My Heart
Where Love Prevails, a Magic Art
I Close My Eyes, I am Made Whole
As God's True Love Engulfs My Soul
In My Mind & Three Times Three
I Feel All Love AND Unity.

Forgiveness Prayer – Recite 3X
Purity is My Divine Right
The Force of Calm is in My Sight
The Power of Healing Light Within
Free Forever of Any Sin
I Clear Away All Old Debris
Where Now I Master Destiny.

Health 3X Prayer
My Every Cell in Harmony
My Body Whole Perfect & Free
As Love Lives Strong With ALL Above
My Heart Transcends to Master Love
Where Body and Soul Are Healed & Whole
The Supreme Force Renews My Soul.

Acronyms to Inspire your Subconscious Mind

1. IC – Instead of "I think, therefore I Am", Goddard or a Physicist may say, "I see, therefore, it is"
2. BU – You must be yourself, and become who you were meant to be.
3. UR – You must know that your is-ness is your connection to the universe.
4. CU – You must see yourself as you want to BECOME or HAVE.
5. IB – I become what I think about all day.
6. NU – The power is within when you are aware of your connection.
7. YU – Why NOT you. Your divine inheritance is waiting for you to accept the gift.
8. 6 ¢ - Sixth Sense - Use your inspiration and creative intuition to follow your dreams and manifest your destiny.
9. B4U – You must be "FOR YOU", and mentally a proponent for your self development, self regard and improvement of your life. Be on your own team. Be your own cheerleader. Don't be a mental house divided.
10. BC – You will eventually Be what you see on the picture screen of your mind. Creative visualization is very powerful.
11. URNRG – You are energy. You are pure being. Be aware of your spiritual energetic creative self. Be aware of the signs and symbols of the universe's desire to assist you. You can tap into the unlimited supply of the universe with your awareness of the NOW.
12. CN2BU – Seek inside of yourself. It is an inside job. Look deep within to clear away the past, build yourself up, learn all you can, and take action to be your best so that you may help yourself, your loved ones and humanity.

The 12 Characteristics of Prescient and Prosperous People

1. **A purpose driven personality** with a desire to express themselves in the most constructive ways.
2. **A worldview and consciousness of possibility,** prosperity and harmlessness
3. People who are beyond competitive and very creative. Visionaries who strive to see and feel the reality of their dreams.
4. **Gratitude minded** – people with a thankful heart and sincere belief in the goodness of the universe.
5. **Boldness, action oriented**, willing to take calculated risks, and Authentic.
6. Self Regard – people who believe that they are worthy of a rich and full life and are willing to work to receive it.
7. **At-Ease – Harmonious mind and thinking**. People willing to cultivate peace of mind and balance in body, mind and spirit.
8. **Love of Fellowship** – willing to help others with time and talent.
9. **Receptivity** - Global & Non-judgmental openness to others' ideas and creativity. Open to inspiration.
10. **A Unique Spirit** – Individualization of soul and spirit. Allowing yourself to become who you are meant to be.
11. **Desire to serve humanity** be being your best. A passion to contribute as an individual to the greater good.
12. **Spiritual Awakenings** - People who have become Spiritually Awake to a higher order of being and work to maintain such a level of thinking, acting and being.

How to send and embed ideas in the Subconscious from Conscious. A Short List of Methods and Exercises?

1. Controlled Visualization – Seeing in your minds eye the desired outcome.

2. Affirmations – Speaking and decreeing empowering present tense sentences or words that are in tune with your desired outcome or result.

3. Rituals or Magick? Any ritual, prayer, spell, affirmation, routine, tapping, physical practice, or exercise that energizes the mind toward a specific outcome.

4. Writing Lists and Rereading – Making goal or objective lists to embed in the consciousness what you want and what you want to achieve.

5. Prayers, Prayer Cards, and 3x Prayers – Cards and systematic prayers that can be utilized to energize and unite the reader with the objective or consciousness desired.

6. Symbols, Cards and Staves – Using symbols to embed an idea from the consciousness to the subconscious.

7. Charms or Talismans – Using objects that are meaningful and inspirational for a particular purpose. Also, possessing objects that have been blessed or charged for a particular purpose.

8. Treatments – Prayers and visualizations made on behalf of another to help them or made on your own behalf. Usually made to improve the consciousness of healing and perfection.

9. Acronyms and Chaos Magik – Use of symbols and letters to deeply absorb an idea or to develop a desired power.

10. Symbols – Any written symbol, sticker, tattoo or other picture that may be used to stimulate mind activity regarding the given symbol.

11.   Thankfulness and Humility – Mentally cultivating a open heart and an open mind or emptiness, so that the individual may receive inspiration or gifts.

12.   Psychic Protection Exercises – Doing mental and physical exercises to increase the protection of the mind and body from psychic drain or toxins of others.

13.   Contemplative Action – Maintaining spiritual strength and connection to higher powers and using this connectivity while in action during your daily activities.

14.   Guided Imagery and Guided Meditation – Engaging in mental simulation to experience a desired result or to obtain closure on a past result. Both activities attach meaning to the imagery where meaning can be enhanced in favor of the practitioner.

15.   Feelings – Methods to affect – Intentionally cultivating a particular feeling regarding any issue from past, present or future.

16. Seek inspiration, seek ideas, seek innovation, seek creativity. You can set these intentions in the morning, during the day, and before sleep.

Other Attributes that Affect and Change Belief Structure - Knowledge, Evidence, and Comprehension

1. 5 Senses – What you see, hear, feel, taste, and smell.
2. Experience – What you directly experience or learn about.
3. Change of Environment – The Arrangement of your surroundings of people, places and things.
4. Change of Habits – Restructuring your neuro-pathways.
5. Change in what you are feeding your Mind.- What you read or watch all day long.
6. Lessons - Pain, Pleasure, Authority – Physical training such as military or athletics where a coach or guru has authority.
7. Memorizing - Active in Action, Passive in Study – Where details are committed to memory.
8. Physical Training in relation to doing. – If you do certain physical activities, you obtain certain results.
9. Reward and Punishment – What you associate pain with, you will be inclined to avoid.
10. Doing Something for the 1st Time, Trying it – Once out of your comfort zone, you see things differently though the pain of going outside of comfort.
11. Awareness - Changing your Perception – Cultivating a mentality of awareness as a seeker of signs and symbols or clairvoyance.
12. Concentration of your mind and body to something specific. – Focusing can make you a specialist.
13. Inspiration or Intuition where you act on Sixth Sense. – Actively seeking inspiration and ideas.
14. Influence of: Respected, Powerful, Peer/Pressure – Looking for higher beliefs from a successful person, guru or person of wisdom.
15. Mindfulness - "Your Clarity of View" affects journey, interpretation, beliefs.
16. Positivity – "Your mental well being" affects the Way you interpret your journey. – If your spiritual self is healthy, you will perceive events in their clearest and highest form.

The Elemental Mind and Body

It is somewhat essential to know that we are not merely this visible body, but have a vital body to charge it with energy, a desire body to spend this force, a mind to guide our exertions in channels of reason, and that we are virgin spirits enmeshed in a threefold veil as egos.

It is also interesting to contemplate that the physical body is the material counterpart of the Divine Spirit, that the vital body is a replica of the Life Spirit, and that the desire body is the shadow of the Human Spirit, the mind forming the link between the threefold spirit and the threefold body.

Even when a seeker analyzes the various cultures around the world, you may find that the soul, mind, self, and spirit may be made up of various parts.

"I AM NOT MY EGO" is a saying that most of us would agree with. There is something deeper – Something in the Heart that you might refer to as "ME," or your higher spirit.

As with Ancient Shamanic Faiths, the soul or spirit is an inherently complex manifestation. We will not go into depth here, but it is important to consider that the spirit includes: Soul Essence, Animating Breath of Life or Silver Chord, The Body Perception, The Shadow Geist, The Hame Skin, The Fetch "Spirit Animal" or Opposite or Feminine, The Mind Emotion, the Memory or Sippe Primal Memories of Ancestry, The Wit which are the 5 Senses of perception, The Will of Boldness and Creation, the Mood of Base Emotions, and the Wode of Higher passions.

In putting this all together, there is the self that wills to survive and attain, the spirit that desires creation and natural expression, and the Mind which assists with memory and function on a conscious and subconscious level.

Many writers have implied that we must maintain balance with the various parts of our soul, self, and mind much like we maintain balance with Body, Mind and Spirit. Some writers refer to the Vital or Elemental body as the part of you that serves you in many ways with confidence, creation, support and energy. Much like an imaginary childhood friend, this vital or elemental body is always there to help you, meet with you, talk with you, and assist you. It is your job to nurture it and keep it healthy. [i]

The Mind of Wonder and Awe

Awe and wonder are things that we perceive that are not typically in the five senses of taste, feel, smell, sound, and seeing, so we actually can experience something without a tangible comprehension. So, awe is also part of an extra-sensory perception, along with empathy as well. Since emotions are based on perception, there is something beyond the mere perception that causes a varying emotions.

The next section is about prayer and meditation, communing with the spirits and with God. A trance state, a meditative state, and the essence of the search for Maximum Peace/Awareness is to maximize consciousness of life, abundance, aliveness, potential, and awareness. If we can operate from a higher order of perception, our view and journey are optimized. Further, a higher consciousness allows a greater connection prescience, and imagination, which can be utilized upon our inner and outer worlds. We have to be contemplative in action, and that is being connected to the universe, while being conscious of what is going on which, in essence, taps us into a higher grade of thought and insight.

In every culture there are different parts of the body from the crown at the top of your head to your heart to your throat down to your stomach and lower chakras and to your feet that ground you to the earth. All of these are interesting aspects of your body and yourself, which could be equated to aspects or facets of the soul as well.

Here is a short list of things or issues that may affect consciousness that may be beyond the normal 5 senses. Ways to alter consciousness and thinking.

1. There is the breath or the breath of life, and how the air itself you breath and the contents of that air can affect you and the quality of the air can affect you.

2. There are exercises and poses and different routines for the body to be stretched or strengthened.

3. There is nature and earth and how to commune with nature and the earth, whether it is outward bound or a vision quest, or anything else.

4. There are the five elements. How earth, wind, fire and ice, or a fifth element such as the all permeating ether that is in the interspaces of the universe.

5. The of course, diet and nutrition affects your consciousness and your perception of life.

6. There is also fellowship with others and whom you associate with, who you talk to, what you verbalize, what you hear and listen to—how that energy or vibration affects your consciousness.

7. Lists and objectives alter your consciousness. If you write a journal or make a list or add goals to the list, how does that change your focus and your intention, and how you put things in order in your life—the order in which they are important.

8. There are environmental issues, the people, the placed, and the things and the arrangement of energy and objects around you. Whether order changes your consciousness

9. The teacher and a guru relationship is an affect. If someone who is your trusted advisor, how does that affects your consciousness and your growth and your human potential.

10. How you speak is an affect. Your incantations and decrees, and affirmations and what you say and what you repeat out loud or in prayer, how that would affect your mental consciousness.

11. Applied meaning or your past. This raises the question of how your past or your childhood, and how your ancestors and elders all affects your karma, circumstances, luck, and your reaping and sowing of life.

12. How you utilize imagination and how to use exercises of imagination to expand your consciousness.

13. Neuroplasticity. Really about changing or reprogramming the way you think about your competencies.

14. Nootropics. How nutrition and diet and supplements, herbs and other types of regulated intake of chemicals can affect your awareness, function, consciousness, whether they are holistic chemicals or not.

15. Altered states; how some people are just born different. Some people were born really thinking in a vertical way or a horizontal way, and some people have visionary capacities, are more spatial in their mind. And some people who are a little on the edge of either autism or Asperger's or some type of bipolar issues. Sometimes those conditions can allow a person to think both logically, but more importantly in a non-logical way,

which allows them to think outside of what the normal people are confined to.

16. Inner Gravity? And then the last issue is just the inner ear. How the compass or gravity of your inner body can affect you, and what that is. Everyone has an inner ear situation where it could be adjusted if necessary.

Here are some steps that most people may find necessary to innovate, grow, expand, improve, or even heal.

1. A burning desire supported by real facts.
2. Repairing error thought – incorrect human beliefs about self and others.
3. Writing out or discussing what you really want to do with your life.
4. Humility and a willingness to listen and learn (teach-ability)
5. Ability to rise above the challenges & to forgive self and others
6. An ability to do what it takes to transcend above challenges.
7. A clear comprehension of the benefits of change, the sacrifices needed to transcend, and the pain associated lack of change.
8. Moving toward Natural Expression of what you life was meant to be.

Other points that groups such as EST and The Course in Miracles espouse are how we interpret the MEANING of the past. Also with the 12 steps, Mind Science, and therapeutic organizations, the issues of character analysis, making and discussing an inventory of past, and working through the details of your memories, experiences, fears and resentments are key to growth. Those who can take a hard look at themselves and experiences and learn from them are the people who can grow. Those who can look at one part of the past as an experience that does not totally define them will also grow. Those who can purge thoughts of anger, fear or resentment to obtain purity of thoughts and freedom of mind will have peace. In sum, a person who is willing to look at their part and involvement in the past, discuss it, and pray for release from the bond of the past will be liberated.

The 12 Step Philosophy that is credited to Bill Wilson and Dr. Bob Smith was quite innovative also. With the influences of people like Fr. Ed Dowling and Dr. Sam Shoemaker, the 12 steps suggest that you have a God of Your Own Understanding. Therefore, this method virtually eliminated dissent because each person could find their own unique God or Higher Power and develop a personal and direct relationship without a middleman. Those who simply can't get to the point of "God" or "Higher Power" Belief or observance are encouraged to allow the conscience of the group or the power of the principles/primary purpose to be their "Higher Power". GOD is said to not be a requirement for these programs to work effectively. Those who expand and improve their life are people who work the steps, tackle self-analysis & clean house, make room for good in their life, clear the wreckage of the past, engage prayer and meditation, help others, and grow spiritually. Invariably, all people who are successful are working spirituality in their life in one form or another. Sometimes there are self styled atheists that are successful, and most of them treat the steps or the group force as their "Higher Power". As such, even the Atheist must maintain sufficient humility and "connectedness" to remain successful. Therefore, all prosperous members must avoid "playing God" out of sheer necessity so that they may maintain and achieve peace and harmony.

Steps needed to Make Big Changes

1. The first would be desire.
2. Thought and imagery.
3. Open minded and awareness to change.
4. Planning.
5. Action.
6. Commitment to that action, and earnestness and sincerity.
7. Aim or what is your purpose.
8. Essence. The essence and what's in back of the purpose, such as emotions. And then how you devote your attention and what you are loyal to.
9. Remove or diffuse blocks and obstacles.
10. Connecting with the animating source, and develop a harmonious relationship with the Life Force.
11. Remaining grateful, thankful, and cultivate praise, both for yourself and other people.
12. Be aware of abundance and opportunity and goodness, and how your consciousness in all of that in sum is how your consciousness controls your destiny.

The 12 Step Philosophy that is credited to Bill Wilson and Dr. Bob Smith was quite innovative also. With the influences of people like Fr. Ed Dowling and Dr. Sam Shoemaker, the 12 steps suggest that you have a God of Your Own Understanding. Therefore, this method virtually eliminated dissent because each person could find their own unique God or Higher Power and develop a personal and direct relationship without a middleman. Those who simply can't get to the point of "God" or "Higher Power" Belief or observance are encouraged to allow the conscience of the group or the power of the principles/primary purpose to be their "Higher Power". GOD is said to not be a requirement for these programs to work effectively. Those who expand and improve their life are people who work the steps, tackle self-analysis & clean house, make room for good in their life, clear the wreckage of the past, engage prayer and meditation, help others, and grow spiritually. Invariably, all people who are successful are working spirituality in their life in one form or another. Sometimes there are self styled atheists that are successful, and most of them treat the steps or the group force as their "Higher Power". As such, even the Atheist must maintain sufficient humility and "connectedness" to remain successful. Therefore, all prosperous members must avoid "playing God" out of sheer necessity so that they may maintain and achieve peace and harmony.

Steps needed to Make Big Changes

1. The first would be desire.
2. Thought and imagery.
3. Open minded and awareness to change.
4. Planning.
5. Action.
6. Commitment to that action, and earnestness and sincerity.
7. Aim or what is your purpose.
8. Essence. The essence and what's in back of the purpose, such as emotions. And then how you devote your attention and what you are loyal to.
9. Remove or diffuse blocks and obstacles.
10. Connecting with the animating source, and develop a harmonious relationship with the Life Force.
11. Remaining grateful, thankful, and cultivate praise, both for yourself and other people.
12. Be aware of abundance and opportunity and goodness, and how your consciousness in all of that in sum is how your consciousness controls your destiny.

Spiritual Magic

Various Steps in the Metaphysical and Magical World of Creativity, Good Fortune, Luck, Health, Wealth, and Success

To open this chapter, I want to say that most religions, most spiritual sects, most large organizations, even the Army, the Navy, the Air Force, and the military, all use different forms of rituals, different forms of project management, different forms of organizational charts, sacred symbolism, banners/flags, different ways of getting things done, and various rigid or stylized routines.

The generalized path to getting things done in most large organizations first would be planning. For practical manifesting of goals, you're going to be collecting information based on the goals at hand first. Two, you would be diagnosing the information. Third, you'd be creating a new plan based on the information and the diagnosis. Then you'd be implementing the plan, that'd be step four. And then step five would be continuous improvement or monitoring of the plan.

Okay, that's just five steps for generalized creation or management of projects or tasks to develop a path to get from beginning to end of an objective. Whether you are organizing a wedding or running a foot race, you're going to have to go through these steps. One would be diagnosing your skills; do you need to improve your running, to practice every day, determine how long do you have to practice every day. Implement that regimen and then continuously monitor and improve on that practice. That's just a tiny example used for running or jogging and trying to be healthy.

Now, let's move to the next phase. How do the body, mind, and spirit correlate or cooperate with those five steps. An example, the type of things that would correlate to outcomes would be the law of cause and effect. This law states that the things you put into a idea would affect what you get out of any particular task or plan or mission much like ingredients affect a any recipe. Beyond simple cause and effect, the actual inputs will "Effect your Feelings", your emotions, & how your emotions vibrate on a collective basis. Thus, the totality of your feelings and emotions all day long would be energized by what you ingest: mentally, physically, and spiritually. So, these are just two examples of how: cause and effect modifies emotions and how feelings would affect the five steps of the planning and implementation process of any particular project or task or magical objective. So, the goal of this book really is to move you from complacency to a mindset of: " I've got to work a little magic each day to accomplish more to reach my peak potential." Thus, we are uncovering the secrets that we need to maintain my metaphysical superiority on a daily basis in mind, body, and spirit.

Earth Wind and Fire

To begin with the elements, we have earth or the soil, which is number one. Number two, wind and air. Number three, ice and water. And number four would just be fire, or combustion or creativity. So, these four energies are going to be the main crux of this chapter discussion. Here we will discuss with you how to be a very creative person, to maximize: our innovation, your efficiency, & your productivity so that you may become a powerful individual. To do so, you've got to be in tune with the world and in harmony with the universe. And this also involves not only your body, mind, and spirit but also: earth, wind, fire, ice, and the connective energy that fills the interspaces of the universe. i.e all elements.

If you look at major cultures around the world, they combine these key elements of: earth, wind, and fire, and ice along with the "god force" or Chi/Ki energy that fills all space. The ancients may refer to *ether* which they refer to the energy between and throughout all interspaces of the universe permeating everything.

We're going to focus on: earth, wind, fire, ice and energy and how they relate to us. To put it simply, all of us need to be in tune with the energy around us which includes plants and animals, as best we can. And then the same holds true with the atmosphere and the air that we breathe and to be in harmony with it and then to also be in harmony with the water and ice. So, we have earth, wind, and fire, ice and universal energy to cooperate with on this earthly plane which will assist us in our magical use of mental and spiritual power.

FIRE & HEAT

Many healers, priests, and leaders around the world, use fire with their formal activities. You look at any lodge, temple or cathedral, you're going to see incense and candles and people lighting candles inside the sacred buildings and making prayers to God, a god or a saint. We have seen people using candles, incense and fire in other ways to cast out the old and bring in the new. Some cultures have a festival of lights where they light candles or release illumined-balloons to bring in a new season or a new year. So, whether it's Celtic, Hindu or Asian, it doesn't matter. There are a lot of common denominators around the world with us as human beings needing to maintain our harmony and our relationship with our body, mind, and spirit but also with the world of: "spiritual energies", earth, wind, fire, and ice. Fire symbolized the East, it symbolizes Light, and it is the symbol of Energy.

WATER & ICE

I want to say that with earth, wind, fire and ice that there are rituals practices, and sacraments involved with water that are as old as time, that go back thousands of years. Some of these practices are directly involved with purification which would use water or fire and so forth. If you've seen people being baptized in rivers or people having water thrown on them from a priest or people anointed, there are all different types of purification techniques. Water is symbolized in the West, it purifies, it cleanses, it baptizes, and it feeds us for growth.

EARTH & SOIL

There are still some ancient religions that utilize trees in ceremony, whether it's a very large tree or it could be a piece of wood. It could be in the form of a cross or an ankh or any symbol and that could represent something that brings the initiate closer to the powers of earth or wood. The tree may symbolize growth, a tree of life, the various worlds of a religion, or even be a symbol of worship. All of these things, earth, wind, fire, ice, wood, all of these elemental aspects have meaning in our lives in many ways and can be used in lots of magical areas. Some people do pilgrimages to be in a sacred place which connect them through this earth and to their God. Overall, many people still like to stay connected to earth and nature. Mother Nature is a very awe inspiring world and most people love to see nature and be at one with it. Just to be barefoot with our feet on the ground seems to connect us to this vast and powerful earth. Earth is symbolized by the North, it grounds us, it connects us, and it protects and energizes all.

WIND & AIR

Air is symbolized by the South. Air symbolizes breath, life and birth. Air energizes us and animates us. Air is invisible and takes up space, has volume, and exerts pressure. Air was considered a "pure" element, but in fact the air is made up of a variety of gases, mostly nitrogen and oxygen but includes trace amounts of things like: argon, carbon dioxide, krypton and helium.

We use oxygen to breath from air, then we exhale out carbon dioxide. Further, plants need carbon dioxide to grow and then, plants give off oxygen during photosynthesis. In our first breath, we are alive away from our mother's womb. Air animates our bodies and energizes our soul. We can harness Ki energy from the proper use of air. Air symbolizes intelligence, learning, perception, knowledge, thinking, imagination, travel, creativity, and harmony. Air can be used for good or bad and must be treated with respect. Air is associated with the Spring season and its corresponding direction is East. Wind or Air is the fuel of life itself. It is used to make fire and smoke. Air purifies, energizes, and animates life on Earth.

The Spirit of the Universe, The Force, All Pervading Ether or Ki Energy.

In many cultures, they refer to the universal energy. In Christianity, they may refer to the Holy Spirit. In Ancient written Sumerian texts, KI is the sign for "earth" and the name of a supreme earth goddess who was the consort of An, the sky god. Also, KI Energy is known as the animating unseen life-force within you and throughout the universe. Ki is the universal energy that permeates and penetrates the universe while uniting all things visible or invisible. In Zen or in Japan it is refered to as "Ki" , while China it is refered to as "Chi" or "Qi" and in Sanskrit it is known as "Prana". In ancient Taoism, chi is the god-force that animates the universe. While earth, wind, fire and ice are all important, the Ki "god-force energy" is essential to harmonize your spirit with and to allow yourself to accept life energy, ideas and FLOW from the Ki Force.

Psychic Defense & Talisman and Charms

If you've ever noticed, whether you go to a music show, graduation, or if you're at a religious ceremony, they may have various sacred objects, whether they're used in a ceremony, on top of a altar, or it could be used in a ceremony and in the spiritual and magical world, the same thing. People may use a wand or some type of scepter or jewels. These things have been around for many, many years. Now, even today, I know people that have a favorite watch or carry around a favorite type of stone or have a symbol of a particular saint, man or woman, printed on a coin or on a card that they carry in their wallet or their purse or in their pocket. All of these things are very, very powerful. Sometimes people like to carry around something with a tiny mindful message on it or object containing a written prayer, affirmation or a decree. It could have a picture, like what you may see in holy space, like a saint card. It could have a picture of a saint on one side dedicated to some particular topic. It could be dedicated careers or jobs or employment, like a picture of St.

Joseph on one side and then on the back side, there could be this wonderful prayer or decree asking for help and maintaining harmony with your job and employment world. These types of prayerful tokens have been around forever.

What's very interesting is if you go to a bookstore and buy a particular book, you may find a book about stones or good luck charms and there might be different types of stones that are for good fortune and other types of stones that ward off negative energy. All of these tools are really important and psychologically interesting in the world of magic and spirituality.

Many other people may carry around something that is symbolic of their forefathers or their ancestry. It could be a symbol of their coat of arms or their family crest. It could be a symbol of their family name or religion from their forefathers. The reason that many people do that is it's symbolic of their clan or, in the old Germanic language, they would call it a sippe, symbolic of your soul essence. In some of the ancient Viking literature, you read about a "Fetch" which refers to the animal part of your soul. We might carry around some particular symbol of a falcon or a bear or a lion. All of these images you'll see on family crests. Some Native American mythology contains the same teachings with regard to Fettish or Animal Soul Essence. Similarly, you might also see a person wearing a special pin with their family crest or their family slogan engraved on it. The pin may symbolize their ancestors and it might be written Latin or some other ancient language. These typical objects around the world are very popular and their essence is magical and empowering. People also wear their family colors, tribal colors, or tartan.

I'm just giving you some different ideas about how people use symbols, jewels, talismans or charms. Some people might carry around a lucky object. Some might carry around a picture of something that they consider good fortune or somebody you love may have given you a small gift that you just like to carry around because you believe it projects you.

The most important thing about talismans, amulets and charms is this. You can take one of those objects and you can give it a blessing or you can ask someone to bless it who you believe has spiritual power and skills. Ask someone to bless it as a special object that can protect you, banish evil and harm and provide good fortune for you.

Why are these things important? To be honest, most people are superstitious. Most people do have ideas of what is lucky and what is unlucky based on their life teachings and experience.. They might put on one shoe before they put on the other but the bottom line is most people don't necessarily believe that there are other folks out there putting negative energy on you but the odds are is that type of thing does happen. Within every family dynamic, within every village, within every community and particularly, if you're very successful, you may have people that just don't like you because they're jealous, or they're angry or they're sore that you've become successful and they have not. They might simply be upset because you're happy and they're not or be upset that you've found someone to be with who was special and they haven't found someone. There's a lot of that going around and to be honest with you, rather than take any chances, in this very powerful, energetic world, sometimes it's just downright smart to do certain things to ward off negative energy and ward off negative people. Sometimes you just have to stay away from these people, stay off their radar, because if they're affected by you. They might be thinking about you all day long and you may not even know it. I'm not saying that you should be paranoid. I'm just saying that you should be practical. For you to have yourself immunized, whether you have yourself purified in a Native American ceremony with smoke and a smudge or if you have your home cleansed and purified by a specialist, whether it be a Feng Shui master or a magical healer or a Catholic priest, it doesn't really matter.

The point being is these forces and intentions are real and all of these energies may affect your body, mind and spirit and the four elements around you. That's the key thing is if something can have an effect on you, it might. I'm not saying that you should avoid all challenge and avoid all struggle. That's not the issue. We should always try and better ourselves and be more and go for more and be stronger and wiser. That's not the point I'm trying to make. The point I'm trying to make is we should all do those things but we shouldn't do anything stupid. We shouldn't jump in front of a bullet train because we already know what will happen. By the same token, we shouldn't get into arguments with crazy people because crazy people have nothing to lose but to mess with your energy.

The reason I bring all these things up is if you have the opportunity to stack the cosmic cards in your favor, you may as well do it. I'm not saying you should go to a psychic and have your tarot cards read. I'm not saying that you should go to somebody with a crystal ball to try to have your future read. That's not what I'm trying to say. What we're trying to say is that do the things for yourself and keep the energy for yourself that allows you to feel emotionally happy and to cultivate emotional well being on a daily basis. That includes possessing skills that ward off negative energy and possessing ideas and objects that increase positive energy.

About the Author

Commissioner George Mentz JD MBA CILS is a global entrepreneur trained in international law who has worked or traveled in over 40 nations worldwide. Mentz is an international award winning author and educator based in the United States. Mentz is the first business and law professor in the USA to be multi credentialed in: international law, management consulting, wealth management/financial consulting, and financial planning along with having an earned accredited MBA and JD/Doctor of Jurisprudence degree and USA law license. Mentz has been ranked #2 in the world as a wealth management influencer, and his wealth management handbook has been ranked in the top 100 wealth books of all time.

Counselor Mentz is one of the few in the world who have earned a Doctor of Jurisprudence JD and MBA Masters of Business Administration who has also earned a CILS Graduate Cert./Diploma in International Law. Mentz is the Titular Lord of the Feif of Blondel in Guernsey which is a legally registered Fief that is over 700 years old. Mentz has served as a US Commissioner for the White House Presidential Scholars Program in the USA. Mentz received his DSS Doctor of Spiritual Studies from the Emerson Institute. Mentz established the CWM Chartered Wealth Manager ® educational programs that are offered worldwide.

Bibliography:

Black Elk, N. and Neihardt, J. G. (2000) Black Elk Speaks, Lincoln: University of Nebraska Press.

Capra, F. (1989) The Tao of Physics: An Exploration of the Parallels between Modern Physics and Eastern Mysticism, London: Flamingo

Cleary, T. (1992) The Essential Tao: An Initiation in the Heart of Taoism through the Authentic Tao Te Ching and the Inner Teachings of ChuangTzu, New Jersey: Castle Books.

Collier, R. (1999) The Secret of the Ages, Oak Harbor, WA: Robert Collier Publications

Covey, S. R. (1989) The 7 Habits of Highly Effective People, London: Simon & Schuster.

Drury, Nevill. The Elements of Shamanism. Rockport, Mass.: Element Books, 1989. Eason, Cassandra. The Handbook of Ancient Wisdom. New York: Sterling Publishing, 1997.

Muhammad Al-Ghazzali (1909) The Alchemy of Happiness, trans. Claud Field, London: J. Murray; also at www.sacred-texts.com.

Goleman, D. (1998) Working with Emotional Intelligence, London: Bloomsbury.

Goodwin, Joscelyn. Mystery Religions In The Ancient World. San Francisco: Harper and Row, 1981

Grimm, Jacob. Teutonic Mythology. 4 vols. New York: Dover, 1966.

Franklin, B. (1993) "The Way to Wealth" in Benjamin Franklin: Autobiography and Other Writings, O. Seavey (ed.), Oxford: Oxford University Press.

Heisler, Roger. Path To Power, It's All In Your Mind. York Beach, Maine: Samuel Weiser, 1990

Heschel, A. J. (1975) The Sabbath: Its Meaning for Modern Man, New York: Farrar, Straus and Giroux.

Hill, N. & Stone, W. C. (1990) Success through a Positive Mental Attitude, London: Thorsons.

Hill, N. (1960) Think and Grow Rich, New York: Fawcett Crest.

Hollander, Lee M., trans. The Poetic Edda. 2d ed. Austin: University of Texas Press, 1962.

Jones, Gwyn. A History ofthe Vikings. London: OxfordUniversity Press, 1973

Jung, C. G. (1978) Memories, Dreams, Reflections, Glasgow: William Collins. The Book of Margery Kempe (1936) trans. W. Butler-Bowdon, London: Jonathan Cape.

Krishnamurti, J. (1970) Think on These Things, New York: Harper & Row.

MacGregor-Mathers, S. L., trans. The Book of the Sacred Magic of Abra-Melin the Mage. Chicago: de Laurence, 1932.

Meyer, Marvin W. The Ancient Mysteries: A Source Book. San Francisco: Harper and Row, 1987

O'Donohue, J. (1998) Anam Cara: Spiritual Wisdom from the Celtic World, London: Bantam.

Pirsig, R. M. (1999) Zen and the Art of Motorcycle Maintenance, London: Vintage.

Redfield, J. (1993) The Celestine Prophecy: An Adventure, New York: Bantam.

Schucman, H. & Thetford, W. (1996) A Course in Miracles, New York: Viking

Scovel Shinn, F. (1978) The Secret Door to Success, Camarillo, CA: De Vorss & Co.

Storms, G. Anglo-Saxon Magic. The Hague: Nijhoff, 1948.

Sun Tzu (2002) The Art of War, Denma Translation Group, Boston: Shambhala.

Suzuki, S. (2003) Zen Mind, Beginner's Mind: Informal Talks on Zen Meditation and Practice, New York: Weatherhill, Inc.

Swedenborg, E. (1976) Heaven and Hell, trans. George F. Dole, New York: Swedenborg Foundation.

Teresa of Avila (1989) Interior Castle, New York: Doubleday.

Tolle, E. (2001) The Power of Now: A Guide to Spiritual Enlightenment, Sydney: Hodder.

Tracy, B. (1993) Maximum Achievement: Strategies and Skills that Will Unlock Your Hidden Powers to Succeed, New York: Fireside.

Turville-Petre, E. O. G. Myth and Religion of the North. New York: Holt, Rinehart and Winston, 1964.

Warren, R. (2002) The Purpose-Driven Life, Grand Rapids: Zondervan.

Wiseman, R. (2003) The Luck Factor: Change Your Luck—And Change Your Life, London: Century.

Ziglar, Z. (2000) See You at the Top: 25th Anniversary Edition, Gretna, LA: Pelican Publishing.

---

[i] Supreme Magus - Commentary

www.ingramcontent.com/pod-product-compliance
Lightning Source LLC
Chambersburg PA
CBHW072029230526
45466CB00020B/1144